THE COMPLETE GRIMOIRE OF POPE HONORIUS

THE
COMPLETE GRIMOIRE
OF
POPE HONORIUS

DAVID RANKINE & PAUL HARRY BARRON

Being a partial translation of Wellcome MS 4666,
with numerous additions translated from the French editions of the
Grimoire of Pope Honorius dated 1670, 1760 & 1800,
and a new translation of the German edition of 1845

With introduction and commentary.

Published By Avalonia
www.avaloniabooks.co.uk

Published by Avalonia

BM Avalonia

London

WC1N 3XX

England, UK

www.avaloniabooks.co.uk

The Complete Grimoire of Pope Honorius

This being a partial translation of Wellcome MS 4666, with numerous additions translated from the French editions of the Grimoire of Pope Honorius dated 1670, 1760 & 1800, and a new translation of the German edition of 1845. With introduction and commentary.

ISBN 978-1-905297-65-8

(Paperback Edition)

First Edition, July 2013

Design by Satori

British Library Cataloguing in Publication Data. A catalogue record for this book is available from the British Library.

ACKNOWLEDGEMENTS

We are deeply indebted to Joseph H Peterson for his gracious assistance in providing several of the texts on his outstanding website www.esotericarchives.com, and for supplying the images he reproduced from those texts for use in this book.

We are also indebted to Dan Harms for taking the time to research and copy the material regarding Eliphas Levi's personal notes in his copy of the *Grimoire of Pope Honorius*, and for drawing our attention to the information regarding the murder of Archbishop Sibour in *Encyclopedia of World Crime Vol IV S-Z Supplements*.

Thanks also to Iris Sala for her assistance translating the Latin text and comments on the German text, and Gianluca Perrini for his assistance translating the Italian text; Francis Soghomonian for his comments on some of the more obscure French phraseology; Ioannis Marathakis and Sasha Chaitow for their insight into the Greek seal derived from Paracelsus.

Finally, a huge thank you to Sorita d'Este of Avalonia for her patience and assistance in bringing this work into manifestation.

TABLE OF CONTENTS

INTRODUCTION

The *Grimoire of Pope Honorius* is a significant seventeenth century French grimoire with a selection of Book of Secrets charms attached to it. In combining these two strands of practice, it continued the tradition found in earlier manuscripts where this practice is seen regularly. The word grimoire is derived from the root grammar, and is normally used to represent a *'grammar'* of magic, or workbook of information and techniques. By contrast, Books of Secrets were collections of simple charms using common herbs or household objects, often combined with biblical quotes.

The books or manuscripts commonly known as grimoires were a European phenomena, usually written in the period from the thirteenth to the late eighteenth century. The countries which dominated the Grimoire tradition were England, France, Italy and Germany, with the so-called *'black magic'* grimoires from the end of this period being almost entirely French and Italian. C.J.S. Thompson noted this saying, *"During the seventeenth and eighteenth centuries, several small handbooks were printed and circulated in France and Italy professing to record the true magical ritual."*[1]

Inevitably material crossed borders into other countries, including into Spain, and in the early eighteenth century a compilation text called *Agripa Negra (Black Agrippa)* proliferated in that country. Dedicated largely to treasure-hunting (as much of the Spanish material was, particularly that of the Cyprian textual tradition), this nineteen page collection included several conjurations from the *Grimoire of Pope Honorius*, including the King of the East and the spirit Nembrot (Nambroth).[2] A French version of this text

---

[1] *The Mysteries of Magic*, Thompson, 1927:256.
[2] *Grimoires: A History of Magic Books*, Davies, 2009:114.

called *Agripa Noir* was mentioned in the trial of the Basque cunning-man Gratien Detcheverry in 1750, showing it had returned to the source language it was drawn from.[3]

This process of proliferation is also seen in the nineteenth century German version of the *Grimoire of Pope Honorius* given by Scheible in his *Das Kloster* (1845). This edition has a number of differences to the earlier French versions, including an extra chapter, and all this material has been included as appendixes to this work for the sake of completion, and to highlight the changes found in this process of linguistic and cultural shifts.

Grimoires usually include the creation of the magic circle, consecration of the magic tools, spirit lists (being the angels, demons or other creatures summoned), conjurations of the said spirits, and other correspondences or pertinent information, such as details of purification of the practitioners and their paraphernalia. Some, like a number of the variants of the *Key of Solomon*, replaced spirit lists and conjurations with lists of amulets and talismans, with details of their creation and consecration.

The *Grimoire of Pope Honorius* has never really received the recognition it deserves as arguably the first of the French *'black magic'* grimoires, which are characterised by all being published as *Bibliothèque Bleue de Troyes* (Blue Library of Troyes) works. These widely distributed extremely cheap paperback editions were prevalent across France from the seventeenth to the mid-nineteenth century, and were so called due to the blue sugar paper they were wrapped in.

Despite the tendency to misdate books to attribute greater age to them, we know that there was at least one edition of the *Grimoire of Pope Honorius* published in 1670, as reference was made to it being in the possession of the infamous French sorceress and poisoner La Voisin in 1679. I have examined two different texts dated 1670, which are almost identical, although one has

---

[3] *Cunning-Folk: Popular Magic in English History*, Davies, 2003:174.

some material not found in the other (see the comparison charts for details). The one with less information is found on Joseph Peterson's website, and I have distinguished it with the reference 1670B in this work for convenience.

The first occurrences of other works in this genre are significantly later, thus we see e.g. the *Grimorium Verum* (1817, not the spurious 1517 date on the cover), *Le Grand Grimoire/Le Dragon Rouge* (1750, and mentioned in the 1760 edition of the *Grimoire of Pope Honorius*) and *Le Dragon Noir* (date uncertain, published 1887). It is interesting to note that if the 1629 publication date for the *Grimoire of Pope Honorius* given by Davis (1998:xv), and quoted by Gardner (1959:98) referencing the American anthropologist Charles Godfrey Leland (1824-1903) is correct, it also predates the first known *Lemegeton* (1641).

We can speculate that the *Grimoire of Pope Honorius* does have earlier roots, considering other works named after Honorius exist which predate it by centuries. The Dominican inquisitor Nicholas Eymericus (1320-99) listed a work called Honorius the Necromancer's *Treasury of Necromancy* in his *Directory for Inquisitors* (1376) as one of those he publicly burned.[4] Mesler suggests that this refers to the *Sworn Book of Honorius*,[5] rather than being a different work, but the evidence is lacking for a conclusion either way. The tendency to burn such works as became public has removed many possible sources, as zealous judges and church officials were keen to burn any such necromantic or demonic work *"so that it becomes dust, and so that from it another copy can never be made".*[6] Waite also lists a work entitled *Honorii Papae adversus tenebrarum principem et ejus angelos conjurationes ex originale romae servato* (*[The grimoire] of Pope Honorius against the Prince of Darkness and his angels, conjurations preserved [?] from the Roman original*), which he states was published in Rome in 1529, that he had seen referenced but never actually been able to get hold

---

[4] *Magic in the Middle Ages*, Kieckhefer, 2001:157.
[5] *Invoking Angels, Theurgic Ideas and Practices, Thirteenth to Sixteenth Century*, Fanger (ed), 2012:134.
[6] *Sorcery in Early Renaissance Florence*, Brucker, 1963:19.

of.[7]

The *Enchiridion of Pope Leo III* is probably older than the *Grimoire of Pope Honorius*, although the early date of 1523 is questionable and I have been unable to find any supporting evidence for its existence before 1584. The Book of Secrets section of the *Grimoire of Pope Honorius* refers to the *Enchiridion of Pope Leo III* in several places, indicating it was certainly available before 1670, and not the later 1749 date sometimes quoted. The *Enchiridion* is not a *'black magic'* text, focusing as it does entirely on the Psalms, prayers and charms. Several of the charms in the *Enchiridion of Pope Leo III* are shared with the Secrets text which comprises the second half of the *Grimoire of Pope Honorius*, and the charms in this work also refer to the *Enchiridion* several times. Another *Bibliothèque Bleue* book often classed with these works is *Le Petit Albert* (1702), which is however more accurately a Book of Secrets style text.

Like some other well-known grimoires, *The Grimoire of Pope Honorius* continued an ancient tradition in claiming a prominent figure as its author. However the nineteenth century French occultist Eliphas Levi (1810-1875) took the pseudepigraphical nature of this work seriously, commenting that *"Some old copies of the Grimoire of Honorius bear, however, the name of Honorius II."*[8] The religious Levi observed that *"he decided to become the High Priest of sorcerers and apostates, in which capacity, and under the name of Honorius II, he composed the Grimoire that passes under this name."*[9]

It is possible that the original creator of the *Grimoire of Pope Honorius* was seeking to provide it with a pedigree and provenance by linking it to the earlier 13th century *Sworn Book of Honorius* (also known as *Liber Juratus* or *Liber Sacer*). The work begins with the tale of 811 (or 89 depending on the version) magicians gathering to ensure their knowledge is not lost, and *Liber*

---

[7] *The Book of Ceremonial Magic*, Waite, 1911:89.
[8] *The History of Magic*, Levi, 1913:228. Honorius II was an anti-pope, who sat in opposition to the official pope of the Roman Catholic Church.
[9] *The History of Magic*, Levi, 1913:228-229.

Juratus being the result. This is duplicated in the 1670 version of the *Grimoire of Pope Honorius*, which begins with a similar description of how Honorius called together magicians from all around the world, clearly seeking to link the two works. It must be observed however that this ignores the fact that the Honorius referred to in the *Sworn Book* is called Honorius of Thebes, and is not named as a pope. This Honorius is also called the son of Euclid, linking him to the famous mathematician Euclid of Alexandria (323-283 BCE) who was known as the *'father of geometry'*. Euclid held a fascination for some grimoire magicians, with both Dr John Dee (1527-1608/9) and Thomas Rudd (1583-1665) publishing editions of some of Euclid's mathematical works.

The *Sworn Book of Honorius* dates to the same century as the reign of Pope Honorius III (1148 – 1227), who was the Pope from 1216 to 1227 CE. Before being made Pope, his name was Cencio Savelli, and he was born to a powerful family in Rome. He rose through the ranks of the church, becoming canon of the church of Santa Maria Maggiore, and subsequently the papal chamberlain in 1188 and Cardinal-Deacon of Santa Lucia in Silice in 1193. Cencio became the Cardinal-Priest of Santi Giovanni et Paolo under Pope Innocent III, and significantly became the tutor of the (future) Emperor Frederick II in 1197.

Following the death of Innocent III in July 1216, nineteen Cardinals assembled at Perugia to elect a new pope. The range of problems in Europe at the time combined with worries about a schism in the church led the cardinals to decide on an election by compromise. Cardinal Guido of Praeneste and Cardinal Ugolino of Ostia (who would later become Pope Gregory IX) chose Cencio Savelli, who reluctantly accepted and took the name of Honorius III. At age sixty-eight, Cencio was consecrated as Pope at Perugia on 24th July 1216 and crowned in Rome on 31 August.

As Pope, Honorius III concentrated on two goals, a spiritual reform of the Church, and the recovery of the Holy Land. Unfortunately his attempts to engender a successful crusade failed miserably due to numerous factors, including the vacillation of Emperor Frederick II, insufficient funding and lack of competency amongst both leaders and troops, many of whom were not soldiers.

Honorius III was noted for his kindness and learning, and his influence was felt through his efforts to bring peace and uphold justice across Europe. His patronage of the mendicant orders was expressed through the privileges he bestowed on them, and he approved the Dominicans on 22nd December 1216, the Franciscans on 29th November 1223 and the Carmelites on 30th January 1226. He also canonized six or seven saints, four of whom were English and Irish. These were Saint Benedict of Nursia, the founder of Monasticism, Saint Hugh of Lincoln (Hugh of Avalon), Saint Lawrence O'Toole, Saint Robert of Molesme, the founder of the Cistercians, Saint William of Bourges (William the Confessor), and Saint William of Eskilsoe (William of the Paraclete).

Pope Honorius III was a noted author, who wrote numerous letters in addition to compiling the *Liber censuum Romanae ecclesiae* (Vaticanus 8486), a list of the revenues of the Apostolic See, including donations, privileges granted, and contracts made with cities and rulers. His other writings included biographies of Popes Celestine III and Gregory VII, *Ordo Romanus*, containing various Church rites, and thirty-four sermons. This may be why grimoires were attributed to him, to gain notoriety through connection to a popular and literate pope.

Despite the abuse heaped upon it by the author and mystic A.E. Waite (1857-1942), who described it as *"perhaps the most frankly diabolical of all the Rituals connected with Black Magic"*,[10] the *Grimoire of Pope Honorius* does not degenerate into the pact-mentality of some subsequent grimoires of this genre. This aversion to demonic pacts is emphasised in the 1670 edition of the *Grimoire of Pope Honorius*, where it categorically states, *"Let him not make*

---

[10] *The Book of Ceremonial Magic*, Waite, 1911:265.

any illicit pact with them."

Eliphas Levi's (1810-1875) comments in his writings clearly added to the notoriety of this work, which he also called the *Constitution of Honorius* after the title of one of its sub-sections, stating that *"A man capable of evoking the devil, according to the rites of the Grimoire of Honorius, is so far on the road to evil that he is inclined to all kinds of hallucinations and falsehoods."*[11] However, the religious Levi's negative views of the *Grimoire of Pope Honorius* clearly seem to have been coloured by his own experiences, not so much of the content, but rather of its perceived effect on an unbalanced mind.

In his work *The Key of the Mysteries*, Levi devoted eleven pages to recounting his experiences regarding the murder of the archbishop of Paris, Marie-Dominique-Auguste Sibour (1792-1857), and the role that the *Grimoire of Pope Honorius* played in the murder. Levi recounts that he met a young ecclesiastic at the house of a friend and had serious forebodings about the stranger. The young Priest, Jean-Louis Verger (1826-1857), was described by Levi as, *"a young and slim man; he had an arched and pointed nose, with dull blue eyes ... His mouth was sensual and quarrelsome; his manners were affable, his voice soft, and his speech sometimes a little embarrassed".*[12]

Verger had been sent to Levi by a book-dealer, and was desperate to obtain a copy of the *Grimoire of Pope Honorius*. Levi disparaged the book as worthless, and his cheiromancer friend Desbarroles, who was also present, offered to read Verger's palm. The cheiromantic act was revealing, as it suggested that Verger was a dangerous individual who could easily become a religious fanatic, if he lived much longer, for *'the line of life was short and broken, there were crosses in the centre of the hand, and stars upon the mount of the moon".*[13]

As he departed, the young Priest ominously declared that they would

---

[11] Quoted in Waite, 1897:479.
[12] *The Key of the Mysteries*, Levi, 1959:121.
[13] *The Key of the Mysteries*, Levi, 1959:122.

hear him spoken of before long. The lady who had been their host subsequently revealed that prior to their arrival Verger had revealed his attempted evocation of the devil using a popular grimoire, and his desire to see the devil, who did not appear despite a number of phenomena, including *"a whirlwind seemed to shake the vicarage; the rafts groaned, the wainscoting cracked, the doors shook, the windows opened with a crash, and whistlings were heard in every corner of the house"*.[14] It is perhaps surprising that Verger did not go to an outdoor site such as a forest or ruin as is often advised in the grimoires, rather than trying to call the devil to manifest inside a church, but this may reflect on the state of mind of the Priest!

January 1857 started badly for Eliphas Levi, with nightmares on the nights of the 1st and 2nd about being called to see his dying father (who had died some years previously). On the 3rd January, Levi went to attend the mass for the feast of St Geneviève, patron saint of Paris (and interestingly, one of the few saints mentioned in the charms in the *Grimoire of Pope Honorius*). As the procession arrived, Jean-Louis Verger stabbed archbishop Sibour in the heart with a large Catalan knife crying *"No more goddesses! Away with goddesses!"* This bizarre statement again seems to reflect his unbalanced mental state. Verger was seized and imprisoned, and after being very disruptive during his trial, was executed by guillotine on 30th January 1857.

The information which came to light after his death shed some light on the disturbed mindset of Jean-Louis Verger. He had been banned from the priesthood after a series of failed parish positions. His hostility to archbishop Sibour seems to have stemmed from the archbishop's dismissal of Verger's accusations of homosexual advances from his superior Abbé Legrand. He also attacked the dogma of the Immaculate Conception, ecclesiastical discipline and clerical celibacy.[15]

Some weeks later Levi again met the book-dealer who had sent the

---

[14] *The Key of the Mysteries*, Levi, 1959:123.
[15] *Encyclopedia of World Crime Vol IV S-Z Supplements*, Nash, 1990:2751.

young Priest to him, and the book-dealer informed him that he had sold his last copy of the *Grimoire of Pope Honorius* to Verger. The notoriety and popularity of the *Grimoire of Pope Honorius* had endured for at least one hundred and fifty years at this point, Davies notes that,

> *"From the records the Clavicule of Solomon emerges as the most influential grimoire amongst the Parisian mages ... The Grimoire du Pape Honorius was the next most popular magic book. In 1701 we find a diabolist doctor named Aubert de Saint-Etienne boasting that he possessed copies of both grimoires."*[16]

Another significant owner of the *Grimoire of Pope Honorius* was Catherine La Voisin, the infamous sorceress and poisoner who was involved in the Affair of the Poisons which scandalised the French royal court in 1679. La Voisin, along with her employer, one of King Louis XIV's mistresses, Madame de Mountespan, played the part of altar for black masses performed by Abbé Guiborg, a renegade Catholic Priest. Guiborg had a large collection of grimoires, and additionally *"several grimoires were found amongst the papers of ... La Voisin, amongst them The Book of the Conjurations of Pope Honorius, which contained a series of spells for gambling."*[17]

Levi's experiences clearly coloured his opinion of the *Grimoire of Pope Honorius*, as he also vilified it in *Transcendental Magic*, and recounted a disparaging tale of a workman and his experiences with it in *The Key of the Mysteries*. Both Levi's and Waite's negative comments about the *Grimoire of Pope Honorius* are indicative of the attitude found in the writings of occultists of the nineteenth and early twentieth century's, as seen by Thompson's comments about the *'black magic'* grimoires that, *"all these little treatises are badly printed on poor paper and evidently written by men who had but little knowledge of the subject."*[18]

On examining their content, it is clear that the *Grimorium Verum (True*

---

[16] *Grimoires: A History of Magic Books*, Davies, 2009:96.
[17] *Grimoires: A History of Magic Books*, Davies, 2009:92.
[18] *The Mysteries of Magic*, Thompson, 1927:256.

Grimoire), the *Grand Grimoire* and the *Dragon Noir* all drew heavily from the *Grimoire of Pope Honorius* (as demonstrated in Appendix 1). Where the *Grimoire of Pope Honorius* originally sprang from is uncertain, but it is curious that it should be published in French in Rome, with no trace of the Latin version it was supposedly translated from. Despite the claims of some, it is clear that the *Grimoire of Pope Honorius* pre-dates the *Grimorium Verum*, the latter being dated to 1817 (not the false 1517 date found on the cover). However the *Grimoire of Pope Honorius* can be definitely dated to 1670 and possibly to 1629, making it at least 147 years if not 188 years older than the *Grimorium Verum*. The *Grand Grimoire/Dragon Rouge* also has a spurious publication date on the covers of its editions, of 1421, 1521 and 1522. It is likely that the *Grand Grimoire* followed the pattern of subtracting three (or four) hundred years from its age to look old and authentic, like the *Grimorium Verum*, giving a suggested creation date of 1821/1822. An unsubstantiated date of 1750 has been suggested for the *Grand Grimoire/Dragon Rouge*, but I have not been able to find any substantiating evidence for this claim.

In addition to the *Grimoire of Pope Honorius*, the *Grimorium Verum* also owes much of its contents to the Universal Treatise manuscript family, the third of the four families of *Key of Solomon* manuscripts.[19] Examination of two of the French manuscripts in this family, the late 18th century Wellcome 4669, Book 1 (fo. 77-87) and the 17th century Lansdowne 1202, Book 3 (fo. 105-114) makes it clear how heavily the *Grimorium Verum* draws from them, with much of the material of the first section being near verbatim. The Book of Secrets material which comprises the second half of the *Grimorium Verum* is largely derived from the *Grimoire of Pope Honorius*, as the comparison of content found after this introduction demonstrates.

By contrast the *Grimoire of Pope Honorius* has little common material with any of the *Key of Solomon* manuscripts apart from two of the charms found in the second or *'Secrets'* part. The presence of the *Key of Solomon* can

---

[19] See *The Veritable Key of Solomon*, Skinner & Rankine, 2008:24-25.

be seen, however, in the cover image for the different versions (apart from the 1670 edition) of the *Grimoire of Pope Honorius*, which feature the particularly appropriate lunar pentacle *'For having Familiar Spirits at your Service'*. Some of the versions of this pentacle have a biblical quote from *Hebrews 13:17* around the edge in Hebrew or French, *"Obey your leaders and submit to their authority, for they keep watch over you."*

The *Dragon Noir* (*Black Dragon*) is even more derivative of the *Grimoire of Pope Honorius* than the *Grimorium Verum*. Of the five parts of the *Dragon Noir*, the Evocations, some of the Spells and Counter-spells, the Marvellous Secrets, and the Hand of Glory (but not the Black Hen) are all entirely derived from the *Grimoire of Pope Honorius*. The Black Hen is previously found in the *Grimorium Verum*, making the *Dragon Noir* of little unique value beyond being a historical compilation with a few additional charms included. The first provable date for the *Dragon Noir* is 1887, which is very late. I suspect that it may date to the 1820s-1830s, but have not yet found evidence to support this supposition.

The *Grand Grimoire* (or *Dragon Rouge*) has far less material in common with the *Grimoire of Pope Honorius*, namely a number of the charms found in the latter. Although most of the charms are also found in the *Grimorium Verum*, which could suggest they came second-hand from that work as a source, there is also an interrogation charm unique to the *Grimoire of Pope Honorius* found in the Grand Grimoire, suggesting the charms were drawn directly from it (or possibly an undiscovered intermediate source which duplicates them all).

As you will see in the text of the manuscript itself, the *Grimoire of Pope Honorius* derives some of its content from the *Heptameron* (*'Seven Days'*) of Peter de Abano (1250-1316). This late thirteenth-early fourteenth century text is one of the most significant of all the Grimoires, a manual of planetary magic with the planetary archangels. The *Heptameron* was first published posthumously in 1496, then subsequently published as an appendix to Cornelius Agrippa's (1486-1535) posthumous *Fourth Book of Occult Philosophy* in 1554 (in German), and in Latin in 1600, being subsequently translated into English by Robert Turner in his 1655 edition of the *Fourth Book*. A number of translations into English have been found in manuscripts pre-dating Turner's 1655 edition,[20] so it seems a reasonable possibility that it would also have been translated into French and other languages by practitioners keen to learn from its practices. The conjurations in the *Heptameron* are extremely important, having influenced many subsequent grimoires including the *Key of Solomon*, *Goetia*, and *Grimoire of Pope Honorius* (and hence the *Grimorium Verum*, *Red Dragon* and *Black Dragon*). Included in its contents are the creation of the magic circle, the consecrations of salt, water and incense, conjurations of various spiritual beings, and planetary hours. This is all material which would be repeated and adapted throughout the subsequent grimoires.

As well as material from the *Heptameron*, the content of the *Grimoire of Pope Honorius* also drew on earlier religious influences; in his seminal work on Russian magic, Ryan (1995:295) notes that "*A French Cathar specialist, Rene Nelli, described a very similar prayer current in Languedoc from the twelfth to the twentieth century. It includes Greek and Hebrew words, and Nelli notes that it occurs in the so-called Grimoire of Pope Honorius.*"[21] This refers to the Prayer found on pages 15-16 of the 1760 edition of the *Grimoire of Pope Honorius*.

The spirit names used in the *Grimoire of Pope Honorius* are a mixture of significant previous names and others which do not seem to appear in earlier grimoires. Although they vary, it is worth noting that the spirit list in the fifteenth century *Le Livre des Esperitz* (*The Book of Spirits*)[22] does bear a small degree of similarity to the later *Grimoire of Pope Honorius*, containing the triad

---

[20] See e.g. Sloane MS 3851, reproduced as *The Grimoire of Arthur Gauntlet*, Rankine, 2011, and Sloane MS 3824, part reproduced in *The Book of Treasure Spirits*, Rankine, 2009.

[21] *The Bathhouse at Midnight: Magic in Russia*, Ryan, 1995:295.

[22] Trinity College, Cambridge, MS 0.8.29, fo. 179-182v.

of infernal rulers Lucifer, Beelzebub and Satan (rather than Astaroth) and the four demonic rulers of the cardinal directions. Two of the four names associated with the cardinal directions are the same but transposed on their directional axis, and another one is similar in sound; thus respectively the *Grimoire of Pope Honorius* against the *Livre des Esperitz* has Magoa/Oriens (East), Egim/Amaymon (South), Bayemon/Poymon (West) and Amaymon/Egin (North). The source of these attributions in the *Grimoire of Pope Honorius* is unclear, as those in *Livre des Esperitz* follow the attributions found in earlier sources such as Cecco d'Ascoli's *Commentary on the Sphere of Sacrobosco* (c.1324).

When considering the names of spiritual creatures used in the charms found in the *Grimoire of Pope Honorius*, the influence of Agrippa's *De Occulta Philosophia* may be seen in the charm called *"To make a girl come find you, no matter how wise she may be: operation from a wondrous power from Superior Intelligences"*. The intelligences referred to here are probably the planetary intelligences, as the names of both planetary intelligences (Tiriel for Mercury and Malcha for the Moon) and planetary spirits (Zazel for Saturn and possibly a corrupted form of Bartzabel for Mars) are found in this charm. No earlier source has yet been discovered for the names of these planetary intelligences and spirits, though Nowotny (1949:49) does suggest they may be derived from earlier, as yet unidentified sources.[23]

The *Heptameron* also forms the bulk of the 1744 book *Les Oeuvres Magiques d'Henri Corneille Agrippa* (The Magical Works of Henri Cornelius Agrippa), mentioned in the 1760 edition of the *Grimoire of Pope Honorius*. This book was erroneously described on the cover as being translated by Pierre d'Aban (Peter de Abano). The attribution of de Abano, who is generally credited with being the author of the *Heptameron*, and who died long before Agrippa was born, as the translator of his own work, is a curious

---

[23] *The Construction of Certain Seals and Characters in the Work of Agrippa of Nettesheim*, Nowotny, 1949:49.

mistake, but perhaps was more of a marketing ploy using the more famous (or infamous) magician's name. Certainly there is no material in the book which was actually written by Agrippa at all. A number of the charms found in the *Grimoire of Pope Honorius* are also found in the second part of *Les Oeuvres Magiques d'Henri Corneille Agrippa*, in the section entitled *Occult Secrets*.

There are also numerous charms in the second part of the *Grimoire of Pope Honorius*, emphasising the inclusion of Book of Secrets material, some of which date back to at least the 13th century (e.g. the Letter of St Anthony). The charm entitled *'An Enchantment to Stop Blood'* is previously found in Scot's *Discoverie of Witchcraft* (1584), and was probably copied from this work or some other derivative text. This charm was extremely popular, as it is also found in other works including the Icelandic text called the *Galdabrok*, which was compiled from around 1500-1650.[24] From the mid-16th century there was a huge explosion of Books of Secrets, particularly in Italy and France, which undoubtedly provided much of the material found in later works like the *Grimoire of Pope Honorius*.

The most famous Books of Secrets, an Italian work called *Secreti* by Alessio Piemontese (1500-1566) was astonishingly published in 104 editions in nine European languages between 1555 and 1699.[25] These books were amongst some of the first best-sellers in publishing, containing not only magical charms and spells, but also a diverse spectrum of useful remedies and tips from medical and gardening hints to cosmetics and metalwork!

The charms in the *Grimoire of Pope Honorius* are in two clear sections, starting with the section entitled *'Collection of Some Most Rare Secrets of the Art Magical'*. These are the type of charms frequently found in Books of Secrets, for purposes like healing, winning games, protection in battle and gaining wealth. This is then followed by the section attributed to the Norman magician Guidon, which is either untitled, or bears the title *'Secrets and counter-*

---

[24] *The Galdabrok*, Flowers, 1989:60.
[25] *Science and the Secrets of Nature*, Eamon, 1994:140.

charms by Guidon' or *'Magical secrets and counter-charms'*. Guidon's secrets display a heavy bias towards the protection and healing of farm animals (especially sheep and horses), clearly emphasising his role as a wandering country magician making his living from his charms.

Guidon was literate and drew from other magical works. The charms attributed to Guidon mention several other works, including the *Enchiridion of Pope Leo III*, the *Keys of Solomon* and the writings of Cornelius Agrippa. All of these works predate 1670, placing Guidon in the mid to late seventeenth century.

The French name Guidon is interesting, being that of a small commonly triangular flag carried by cavalry, originating from the Old Provençal word *guidoo*, meaning *'guide'*. There was a Lord Guidon, Archdeacon of Laon, who was a member of the party of Norman clerics who toured Britain in 1113.[26] However a more significant use of the word guidon comes from the *Guidons*, a company of Priests founded in Rome by the Emperor Charlemagne in the early 9th century CE, who conducted and guided pilgrims to Jerusalem, and were charged with healing them if they fell sick and perform the last offices if they died.

To my knowledge, the *Grimoire of Pope Honorius* provides one of the first references to the use of grave dirt in this type of magic. The charm entitled *'To see Spirits, of which the air is replete'*, includes in its ingredients *"some powder from the grave of a dead man, that is to say, some dust, which is touching the coffin"*. As this charm occurs in the earliest available edition, i.e. 1670, it provides us with a date at which time grave dirt is being used in folk magic.[27] Although grave dirt was used in at least one Anglo-Saxon charm, this was a very specific charm for a woman struggling in childbirth, and required the grave dirt from a dead child of hers, and so is based on a specific familial

---

[26] *The Celtic Sources for the Arthurian Legend*, Coe & Young, 1995:47.
[27] This refers to the European use of grave dirt as opposed to African use. There are references, e.g. to the Caribbean dirt oath, requiring the ingestion of grave dirt, from 1750. See Hughes, 1750:15-16.

relationship.[28] Furthermore, the charm *'To use a nail to make someone suffer'* uses coffin nails, which have also become popular against witches and for malicious magic in folk traditions across Europe.

Considering the influence of European grimoiric texts on folk traditions such as hoodoo and Pennsylvania German braucherei, these references hint at a continuity of tradition from the diverse charms of the *Grimoire of Pope Honorius* and its derivative texts into such traditions. However, regarding braucherei, on examination nearly all of the types of charm found in this work are also found in works such as Hohman's *Long Lost Friend* (1820), though they are different examples of such charms, with no duplication between them.

That the charms in the *Grimoire of Pope Honorius* were used in practice is made clear by Meller, who when discussing protective charms placed on weapons, refers to the charm *'Not to be wounded by any weapon'*, when he recounts that *"Such have been found on two swords, one at Lincoln, the other, in France, at St Omer. The words placed on these swords, and, of course, on many now undiscovered, were 'cabalistic,' i.e., the words 'Ibel, Ebel, Abel,' so used."*[29] Of course this also implies that people in England and France were using the material from the grimoire, showing it travelled beyond France and Italy.

In discussing the practices of French charmers, or *panseurs de secret* (healers by secret), Davies notes that *"Chapbook grimoires such as the Enchiridion Pape Léon, Grimoire du Pape Honorious and Le Dragon Noir contained simple healing charms and orisons along with the demonic conjurations for which they were more notorious."*[30] However, magical practitioners in Normandy had to be especially careful, as it was unique in Europe as the only area (not counting Iceland) where the majority of deaths following trials for witchcraft and sorcery were of men. This can be seen from the figures for numbers of men to women

---

28 *The Anglo-Saxon Charms*, Grendon, 1909:209.
29 *Old Times. Relics, Talismans, forgotten customs & beliefs of the past*, Meller, 1925:78.
30 *French Charmers and their Healing Charms*, Davies, 2004:1995.

tried, where the ratio increased from 1.5:1 in the period 1564-78, to 10.5:1 in the period 1646-59.[31] The largest profession group of men tried during this period were shepherds, with Priests coming second with a substantially smaller number, and blacksmiths being the other named group.[32] Both Priests and blacksmiths had a long association with magic, and considering the number of charms for protecting livestock, especially sheep, found amongst Guidon's work, this persecution of shepherds is no surprise.

As might be expected from the material found in the *Grimoire of Pope Honorius* attributed to the Norman magician Guidon, it was a notoriously popular work amongst French sorcerers:

> *"The most extensive diabolical library of which I have read a description was that of Pere Roussel, a sorceror from the commune of Blainville in lower Normandy. He possessed the Oeuvres Magiques de Henri Corneille Agrippa par Pierre d'Alban, avec des secrets occultes (1744) and the Grimoire du Pape Honorius, as well as the Enchiridion. When consulted by the farmer Renoult for his sick cows, around 1837, Roussel proceeded thrice around the stable, reading prayers from the spell-book."*[33]

Clearly the *Grimoire of Pope Honorius* was still popular to some degree in the nineteenth century, as this quote from 1877 from the periodical *The Academy* (12:568) demonstrates, *"As rabbits have become a terrible pest in Australia, it may be worth stating that the Grimoire of Pope Honorius III contains an excellent exorcism against these animals."*[34] This popularity is also reinforced by the playwright Olivia Shakespear (1863-1938), who in her novella *Beauty's Hour*, *"had Dr Trefusis read the Grimoire of Pope Honorius, one of the books [Ezra] Pound suggested Dorothy Shakespear read in his letter about 'symbolism in its profounder*

---

[31] *Toads and Eucharists: The Male Witches of Normandy, 1564-1660*, Monter, 1997, 20:584.
[32] *Toads and Eucharists: The Male Witches of Normandy, 1564-1660*, Monter, 1997, 20:582.
[33] *The Superstitious Mind: French Peasants and the Supernatural in the Nineteenth Century*, Devlin, 1987:167.
[34] *The Academy*, Murray, 1877, 12:568.

sense'. [35]

It is an interesting coincidence that the Irish playwright and magician W.B. Yeats (1865-1939), who was Olivia Shakespear's lover in 1896-97, has his character Hanrahan in his work *The Secret Rose* (1897) connected with the *Grimoire of Pope Honorius*, for *"his tampering with 'the Book of the Great Dhoul', the 'Grimoire of Pope Honorius', leads him to trouble in the world of the Sidhe."* [36]

As mentioned previously, it is clear that the charms found in the *Grimoire of Pope Honorius* were used in other derivative works, but the extent to which they spread is sometimes surprising. Writing on invisibility spells, the scholar Ioannis Marathakis notes that *"The infamous French Grimoire of Pope Honorius contains a recipe very similar to the first two Greek versions [found in the 19th century Bernardakean Magical Codex]."* [37]

Another significant influence of the *Grimoire of Pope Honorius* may have been on the development of the tradition of initiatory Wicca publicized by Gerald Gardner (1884-1964) in the 1950s. In *Wicca Magical Beginnings* (2008), Sorita d'Este and I discussed at length aspects of Wiccan practice which appear to have been influenced by the *Grimoire of Pope Honorius*. [38] These include the creation of the magic circle using spoken words, the conjuration of spiritual creatures at the cardinal points and their dismissal at the end of the ceremony, and the use of the black-handled knife (also found in the Key of Solomon and other texts). Gardner himself refers to owning a copy of this work (1959:98), writing *"We have a copy of The Grimoire of Honorius in the Museum"*,[39] and also mentions it in his previous work *Witchcraft Today* (1954), which first announced Wicca to the world as a living tradition. That both Gardner's works on witchcraft and Wicca mention the *Grimoire of Pope*

---

[35] *Stone Cottage: Pound, Yeats & Modernism*, Longenbach, 1988:83.
[36] *Reconstructing Yeats: The Secret Rose and The Wind Among the Reeds*, Putzel, 1986:75.
[37] *From the Ring of Gyges to the Black Cat Bone - A Historical Survey of the Invisibility Spells*, Marathakis, 2007.
[38] *Wicca Magical Beginnings*, d'Este & Rankine, 2008.
[39] *The Meaning of Witchcraft*, Gardner, 1959:98.

Honorius and the *Key of Solomon*, the two most obviously influential grimoires on Wiccan practice, is surely no coincidence.

Through its different editions, its influence on other grimoires and on magical traditions in the last three centuries, it is clear that the *Grimoire of Pope Honorius* is actually one of the more significant grimoires. This work aims to redress the balance and demonstrate the versatility and significance of this grimoire, cutting past outdated misperceptions to a viewpoint which reflects more accurately the position of the *Grimoire of Pope Honorius* in the development of magic since the seventeenth century.

David Rankine

May 2013

GRIMOIRE OF POPE HONORIUS: TIMELINE TO THE LATE 19TH CENTURY

Date	Language	Text
13th Century	Latin	*Sworn Book of Honorius* first appears
1496	Italian	First publication of the *Heptameron* in Venice
1523*	Italian	*Enchiridion of Pope Leo III* allegedly printed in Rome
1584	English	*The Discoverie of Witchcraft* by Reginald Scot
17th Century	French	*The Clavicles of King Solomon by Armadel* (part of the Armadel Text Group of KoS MSS), bound with *The Book of Gold*[40] Lansdowne 1202
1629*	Italian*	*Grimoire of Pope Honorius* allegedly printed in Rome
1633	Italian	*Enchiridion of Pope Leo III*, first verified edition
1641	English	*Lemegeton* Sloane 3825
1670	French	*Grimoire of Pope Honorius* printed in Rome, there seem to be two editions, referred to in the text of this work as 1670 and 1670B
1723*	Spanish	*Agripa Negra* in circulation, date uncertain
Mid-18th Century	French	*Grimoire of Pope Honorius*, bound with *Key of Solomon* and *Grand Grimoire* Wellcome 4666
1744	French	*Les Oeuvres Magiques d'Henri Corneille Agrippa* published
1750	French	*Agripa Noir*, the French version of *Agripa Negra*, mentioned in the trial of Gratien Detcheverry
1750*	French	*Le Grand Grimoire/Veritable Dragon Rouge* allegedly published

---

[40] See *The Book of Gold*, Rankine & Barron, 2010

1760	French	*Grimoire of Pope Honorius* (BL 8632.a.3.)
1796	French	*The Keys of Rabbi Solomon* (part of the Rabbi Solomon Text Group of KoS MSS, includes charms found in *Grimoire of Pope Honorius* in Wellcome MS 4666 and 1800 edition) Wellcome MS 4669
1800	French	*Grimoire of Pope Honorius* (BL 8630.aa.21.)
1817	French	*Grimorium Verum* Alibeck edition
1821	French	*Le Grand Grimoire/Veritable Dragon Rouge* published
1825	French	*Dictionnaire Infernal* by de Plancy published
c.1830	French	*Grimorium Verum* Blocquel edition
1845	French	*Le Grand Grimoire* Venitiani edition
1845-49	German	*Der Gross Grimoir Des Papis Honorius* Das Kloster
1868	Italian	*Grimorium Verum* Bestetti edition
1880	Italian	*Grimorium Verum* Muzzi edition
1887	French	*Dragon Noir* published.

COMPARISON OF
CONTENT IN DIFFERENT EDITIONS

	Grimoire of Pope Honorius III					
	1670	1670B	Mid C18	1760	1800	1845
Constitution of Pope Honorius III	1-14			3-15	1-13	Yes
The 72 Names of God	14-15			15-16	13	
Gospel of St John	15-17		203-204	16-18	14-16	
The Universal Conjuration	17-19	Yes	185	18-19	16-18	Yes
Conjuration	19-21			20-22	18-20	Yes
Discharge of the Spirits	21			22	20	Yes
Conjuration of the Book	22	Yes	184-185	22-23	21	Yes
It is necessary to say that which follows before the sealing of the Book	22-24		186	23	21-23	Yes
Conjuration of the demons/Air Spirits*	24-25	Yes	186	24-25	23	Yes*
The Figure of the Circle represented to the side and that which concerns it	25	Yes	186	25-26	24	Yes
That which needs to be said when forming the Circles	25-27	Yes	187-188	26-27	24-26	
Discharge of the Spirits	27-28	Yes	188	27-28	26	
Conjuration of the King of the East	28-29	Yes	189	28-29	26-27	Yes

Conjuration of the King of the South	29	Yes	189	29	27-28	Yes
Conjuration of the King of the West	29-30	Yes	189	29	28	Yes
Conjuration of the King of the North	30-34	Yes	189-191	30-34	28-33	Yes
Conjuration of the Kings of the South			191			
The characters represented below are those of the Spirit of Darkness, Leviathant			191-192			
The characters of the Spirit, who is called Berith			192			
Conjuration and Evocation to Belzebut			192-193			
Conjurations for each day of the week	35	Yes	193	34	33	Yes
For Monday to Lucifer	36-37	Yes	193-194	34-36	34-35	Yes
For Tuesday to Nambroth/Frimost*/Nimrod**	37-38	Yes	194-195	36-37*	35-36	Yes**
For Wednesday to Astaroth	38-40	Yes	195-197	37-38	36-38	Yes
Conjurations			197-198			
Discharge of the Spirits, whilst in the Circle			198-199			

For Thursday to Acham/Silcharde*	40-41	Yes	199	38-39*	38-39	Yes
For Friday to Bechard/Bechet*/Ragiel**	41-42*	Yes	199-200*	39-40	39-40	Yes**
For Saturday to Nebirots/Guland*/ Nabara**	42-44	Yes	200	40-42*	40-41	Yes**
For Sunday to Surgat/Acquiot*41/Aquiel**/Aziel***	44-50*	Yes	200-201**	42-43	41-43**	Yes***
Very Powerful Conjuration for all days and all hours, Day and Night, for treasures hidden by men as well as Spirits, to have them or have them transported		Yes	201-203	43-47	43-47	Yes

41 The less complete version 1670B text has Acquiot here, whereas the more complete version has Aquiel but combines the conjuration with the following Very Powerful Conjuration.

Charm	Collection of Some Most Rare Secrets of the Art Magical					
	1670	1670B	Mid C18	1760	1800	1845
To see spirits, of which the air is replete	50-51	Yes		48	47-48	
To make three ladies or three gentlemen come to your room after supper	51-54	Yes			49-51	
To make a girl come find you, no matter how wise she may be	54-57	Yes			51-54	
To win at games	57	Yes		48	54	
In order to extinguish a chimney fire	57	Yes		48	54	
To make oneself invisible	58-69	Yes			55-56	
To get gold and silver, or a Hand of Glory	60-62	Yes		48-51	57-59	
Garter in order to travel without tiring oneself / To succeed on a journey*42	62-64*	Yes		51-53	59-61	
To be hard against all manner of weapons	64-65	Yes		53-54	61-62	
Conjuration to the Sun / To see someone far away*	66*	Yes		54	62	
To make a person come to you	66-67	Yes			63	
To make a girl dance naked	67	Yes			63-64	
To see a vision in the night of what you wish to see, in the past or the future	68-69	Yes		54-55	64-65	

---

42 All of the alternative titles in the 1670 column for charms refer to the incomplete version of the text, not the complete one.

To use a nail to make someone suffer	69-70	Yes		55-56	65-66	
To prevent a person from sleeping the whole night	70-71	Yes			67-68	
To make oneself appear to be accompanied by many	72	Yes		56-57	68-69	
Not to be wounded by any weapon	72-73	Yes		57	69	
To enjoy the use of whomever you wish. Secret of Father Girard	73	Yes			69-70	
To make a weapon fail	74	Yes		57-58	70	
For Pleurisy	74	Yes		58	70	
For fevers / For all fevers*	74*	Yes		58	70	
For intermittent fever				58		
For tertiary fever				58-59		
For quartan fever				59		
To stop loss of blood	74	Yes		59	70	
Against a sword strike	74	Yes		60	71	
For when you are going into action / To be sheltered from all nasty action*	75*	Yes		60-61	71	
To extinguish fire / To extinguish interior fire*	75-76*	Yes		61	72	
For burns / To heal a burn*	76*	Yes		61-62	72	

For headaches	76	Yes		62	72	
For Stomach Flux / To stop the flux*	76-77*	Yes		62-63	72-73	
To prevent [someone]* from eating at the table	77*	Yes		63	73	
To extinguish fire	77	Yes		63	73	
To prevent copulation	77	Yes		63-64	73-74	
For Games / To win at games*	78*	Yes		64	74	
To stop a serpent [in its tracks]*	78*	Yes		64-65	74	
To prevent a dog from barking and biting	78-79	Yes			75	
For ringworm of the hair	79	Yes		65	75	
For games of dice	79	Yes		65-66	75-76	
To remove a fish-bone from the throat	80	Yes	.	66	76	
Not to tire of walking	80	Yes		66-67	76	
To win at all games	80	Yes		67	76	
To avoid undergoing interrogation	80-81	Yes			76-77	
Secrets and counter-charms by Guidon / Magical secrets and counter-charms*	81*	Yes			77	
Guidon's practice when it concerns dispossessing [/when it is a matter of destroying a cure placed on a human being or an animal]*	82-83*	Yes			78-79	

To break and destroy all evil spells / Another, to destroy all curses affecting animals*	83*	Yes		67	79	
The Great Exorcism to dispossess either the human creature or irrational animals	84-89	Yes		68-72	80-84	
To remove all spells and to summon the person who caused the evil deed	89-92	Yes		72-75	85-87	
The Castle of the Fair, a guard for horses / Secret to destroy the bewitchment cast upon the animals, in particular horses and sheep*	92-98*	Yes		75-81	87-93	
Guard for whatever you will / Another secret to break a spell*	98-99*	Yes		81	93-94	
Another guard / Against cast lots, another very effective secret*	99-100*	Yes		81-82	94-95	
Guard [or protection]* against mange, scabies and sheep-pox	100-103*	Yes		82-84	95-97	
Guard against mange / Another secret for healing*	103-104*	Yes		85	97-98	
Guard for preventing wolves from entering into a field where there are Sheep	104-105	Yes		85-86	98-100	
The Marionettes of Protection	105			87	100	
Guard for horses / Protection for horses against all cast lots*	105-106*	Yes		87-88	100-101	
Guard for the flock / Protection of a flock*	106-109*	Yes		88-90	101-103	
Another Guard [Protection]* for sheep	109-111*	Yes		90-91	103-106	

New Guard for sheep, taught by the learnèd Bellerot, in his treatise on the preservation of woolly beasts		Yes		91-93		
Guard against [the damages caused by]* rabbits	111-115*	Yes		93-96	106-109
To control [an animal]	115	Yes			109
To be hard / To escape all attack, no matter how violent it may be*	116*	Yes			110
[Secret]* To discover treasures	116-117*	Yes			110-111
To stop horses and carriages / To tame malicious horses*	117-118*	Yes		96-97	111-112
Counter-Charm	118	Yes		97-98	112
For the lambs to return beautiful and very strong / Against all charms affecting animals*	118*	Yes		98	112
Against firearms / Protection against all firearms*	119*	Yes		98-99	112-113
For ulcerous lesions	119	Yes		99	113
For glanders and colic in horses / For all manner of sicknesses in horses*	120*	Yes		99-100	113-114
To heal sprains and twists in horses [/in men and in animals]*	120	Yes		100-101	114*
To prevent a flock from touching [a harvest]* the grain, passing between two furrows	121*	Yes		101	114-115
To heal a beast afflicted with haemorrhaging	121	Yes		102	115

For growths or asthma	122	Yes			115
For mumps	122	Yes		102	115
For scabies and ringworm in animals/mange*	122*	Yes		102	116
For hæmorrhoids	123	Yes		102-103	116
For epilepsy or falling sickness	123	Yes		103	117
Enchantment for stopping blood	124	Yes			117
Counter charm	124	Yes			117
Against fire	124	Yes			117
For fevers / Cure for fevers*	124-125*	Yes			118
Some more precious additions					
For dropsy				109	
For cuts				109-110	
For iron splinters that have entered into the eyes				110-111	
For white finger				111-112	
For haemorrhages and blood loss				112-114	
For Relentless Diarrhœa				114	
Correspondences of ancient weights with decimal weights				115	
Table of medication doses				116	

THE VERITABLE

GRIMOIRE OF

POPE HONORIUS

(TRANSLATED FROM WELLCOME MS 4666)

(183)[43]

THE VERITABLE GRIMOIRE OF POPE HONORIUS

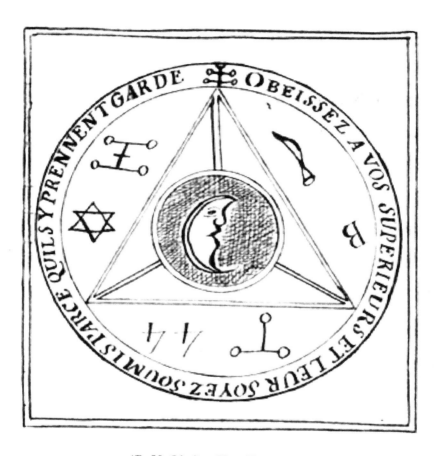

*"Be Ye Obedient Unto Your Superiors
And Submit To Them For They Are Mindful Thereof"*

---

[43] Editors' Note – the figures in brackets through the texts indicate the page numbers in the original manuscript or book.

The Operator in his Circle

Ready To Appear (184)

CONJURATION FOR THE BOOK, which should be said before using it:

"*I conjure thee, Oh BOOK to be useful and profitable unto all those who shall read thee for success in their affairs. I conjure thee, anew, by the virtue of the Blood of Jesus Christ that is daily contained in the Chalice, to be of use to all those who shall read thee. I exorcise thee, in the Name of the Most Holy Trinity, in the Name of the Most Holy*

Trinity, in the Name of the Most Holy Trinity."

For any operation that you wish to perform, it is important to take the Intelligence of the Kingdom into consideration. The Intelligence that rules and governs France is called ACHEL.

"I conjure thee, Achel (likewise, the Intelligence of the Month) and also the Spirit of the Day.... I conjure thee, N. by the Great Living God, who is thy master and mine and by the great Names of God JEOVA[44] &c. And by the Powers of the Heavens, the Earth and the Waters and by the Power that God hath given thee, that thou beest favourable unto me in the work that I shall undertake, which is to invoke N.. I conjure thee to compel them to come and speak unto me and to obey me, those, who are under thy power, so that I may be completely satisfied by thy favour and by the power of the Intelligences, which I invoke, all to the Glory of God, Our Creator."

The appropriate times for the Conjurations following flagellation are those for the Conjurations of Dæmons. Suitable days fall on the Eve of each of the Four Great Festivals of the Year, as well as the Festivals of the Holy Virgin;[45] the Ember Days are also most suitable. For the times and hours when Devils appear, see Book 4, Chapter 14 page 357 on The Apparition of Spirits[46] and in J. Bellot[47] at the section on the 4th Commandment of God given to Moses, page 47.

As far as the Pentacle is concerned, you should also take heed that it is to be made on Virgin Parchment, as is also the card or list. You can buy Virgin Parchment and bless and exorcise it according to the Art; it should be made from Vellum, Deerskin or Lambskin &c.

ORATION AND PREPARATION FOR THE WORK

"Atrachios, Asach, Asarca, Abeda, Mabas, Silat, Anabolas, Jesibilin, Seigim,

---

[44] An alternative spelling of Jehovah from the Hebrew יהוה.
[45] There are 19 Feast Days dedicated to the Virgin Mary.
[46] *"Traicté de l'apparition des esprits"* [Treatise on the Apparition of Spirits] by Capuchin monk Noël Taillepied (1540-1589), 1588. The chapter is actually 15, not 14.
[47] This might refer to Jacques Bellot, the *"gentleman originally from Caen"*, Normandy, who taught French in London, where he had sought refuge for religious reasons from 1580 to 1590. He was principally famous for his language teaching methods and author of the book *The French Method* (1588). However, *'Bellot'* might equally refer to Jacques Bellot, who was the Parish Priest of Charleval in the Normandy region of Eure in 1643 and there seem to be a lot of connections with Normandy.

Jeucon, Dontol."[48]

You may then perform any other prayer in accordance with your will.

Take heed that it may be better to make the character for Scirlin with your own Blood. (185)

NAMES, QUALITIES AND PLACES, WHERE THE INFERNAL INTELLIGENCES RESIDE AND THE NAMES THAT ARE SUPERIOR TO ALL THE OTHERS.

LUCIFER   Emperor, His Subjects Dwell in Europe.
BELZEBUTH   Prince, His Subjects Dwell in Asia.
ASTAROTH   Count, his Subjects Dwell in the Americas.
NAMBROTH   Baron, His Subjects Dwell in Libya[49] and Mount Etna.

UNIVERSAL CONJURATION

"I, N. do conjure thee Spirit N. in the name of the Great Living God, who hath made the Heavens and the Earth and all those that are contained therein; and by virtue of the Holy Name of J.C. His most beloved Son, who did suffer Death and Passion for us on the Tree of the Cross and by the precious love of the Holy Spirit, Perfect Trinity, to appear before me in a human and fair guise, without creating fear, nor noise and without causing any fright whatsoever. I, therefore, conjure thee in the Name of the Great Living God ADONAY, Tetragrammaton, Jehova, Otheos, Athanatos, Ischiros,[50] Agla, Pentagrammaton, Jehova, Ischiros, Athanatos, Adonar, Jehova, Otheos, Saday, Saday, Saday, Jehova, Otheos, Athanatos, Tetragrammaton, to Luciat, Adonay, Ischiros, Athanatos, Saday, Saday, Saday, Adonay, Saday, Tetragrammaton, Saday, Jehova, Adonay, Ely, Eloy, Agla, Eloy, Agla, Ely, Agla, Agla, Agla, Adonay, Adonay, Adonay, come N., come N., come N.. I conjure thee, anew, to appear before me by the aforementioned virtues of the powerful and sacred Names of God that I have presently recited in order to achieve my desires and wishes, with no falsehood nor lies. Or else, may the Holy Invisible Archangel Michael smite thee into the deepest of Hells. Therefore, N., come do my will."

---

[48] Cf. *Grimorium Verum* Chapter 5.
[49] '*Libya*' in Classical Greek terms referred to the whole of North Africa, from Morocco to the Western part of the Nile Valley.
[50] A number of these divine names and the sequence indicate the influence of the conjurations from the *Heptameron*.

That, which needs to be said before the sealing of the BOOK[51]

"*I conjure and command you, Oh Spirits, all and so many as ye are that ye receive this* **BOOK** *graciously, so that when-soever we shall read from the said* **BOOK**, *or anyone reading it, being approved and recognised to be in good stead and worthy, ye shall appear in a comely human guise, when ye are called upon, according to the judgement of the reader. In no circumstances shall ye make any attempt upon the body, soul or (186) spirit of the reader; neither shall ye harm those, who may accompany him, whether through mutterings, through tempests, noises, thunderbolts, scandals, or through injury, nor prevent the execution of the commandments of the book. I conjure you to come as soon as the conjuration hath been made, so that ye may execute without delay all that is written and mentioned in its proper place in the said book. Ye shall obey, ye shall serve, ye shall instruct, ye shall impart, ye shall do all that is in your power, whilst being of assistance to those who command you in all without illusions; if by any chance, one of the called Spirits be not able to come or appear when he is called, he will be bound over to send others, assuming his power, who will swear to solemnly execute all that the reader may demand; ye are all hereby enjoined by the Most Holy Names of the* **Almighty Living God Eloym, Jah, El, Eloy, Tetragrammaton**, *to do all that is said here-above. If ye obey me not, or if one of you doth not receive this Book with complete resignation to the will of the Reader, I shall compel you to walk in sorrows for a thousand years.*"

CONJURATION OF DÆMONS

"✝[52] *In the Name of the Father and of the Son and of the Holy Spirit. Take Heed! Come all ye Spirits by the virtue and the power of your King and by the seven crowns and chains of your Kings, all the Spirits of the Hells shall appear to me, before this circle, when-soever I shall call upon them.[53] Having been commanded, come all ye at my commandments to do all that is in your power. Come, therefore, from the East, South, West and from the North. I conjure you and command you by the virtue and power of The One who is Three, Eternal, Equal, who is God, invisible, consubstantial, in a word, He who hath created Heaven, the Sea and all that is under the Heavens.*"

After these conjurations, you will order them to affix their Seal.

---

[51] Some authorities state that this involves the Spirit sealing or '*signing*' the Book, promising to return, when called upon.

[52] + indicates that the '*Sign of the Cross*' is to be made. This is true for all occurrences in the entirety of this book.

[53] This version omits "*are forced to appear in my Presence before this Pentacle or Circle of Solomon*".

THE FIGURE OF THE CIRCLE REPRESENTED TO THE SIDE AND THAT WHICH CONCERNS IT.

These Circles must be made with charcoal and sprinkled with holy water or with the wood from the blessèd Cross. When they have thus been made and when the words have been written around the Circle, the holy water, which shall be used to bless the circle may be used to prevent the Spirits from causing harm. And when you enter into your circle, you will command them with authority and vivacity, as one who is their Master.

THAT, WHICH NEEDS TO BE SAID WHEN FORMING THE CIRCLES (187)

"Oh Lord, we appeal unto Your[54] virtue. Oh Lord, confirm this work, which is being manifested within us, becoming as dust in the wind, with the Angel of the Lord stopping the Darkness from disappearing and the Angel of the Lord ever pursuing Alpha, Omega, Ely, Elohe, Elohym, Zebahot, Elion, Saday; Behold the Lion, who is the conqueror of the Tribe of Judah, the Root of David.[55] I shall open the Book and the Seven Seals.[56] I have beheld Satan as a light falling from Heaven.[57] It is You, who hath given us the power to trample the Dragons, Scorpions and Your enemies under Your feet. Naught will harm me,[58] not even Eloy, Elohym, Elohe, Zebahot, Elion, Esarchie, Adonay, Jah, Tetragrammaton, Saday.[59] The Earth and all those, who dwell therein are of God, because He hath established it upon the seas and He hath prepared it upon the rivers. Who is the one who shall ascend upon the mountain of the Lord? Or who is he who shall not be received in His Holy Place? The innocent of hand and the pure in heart! Who hath not received his soul in vain and who hath not borne false witness to his neighbour? The same shall be blessed by God and shall receive God's mercy unto his salvation. He is of the generation of those, who seek him. Princes, open your Gates, open the Eternal Gates and the King of Glory shall enter! Who is this King of Glory? The

---

[54] You would expect the *"Tu"* (*"Thou"*) to be used here, as in other Ecclesiastical and Magickal works, but the text employs the *"Vous"* (*"You"*, polite form, or even plural *"you"*) instead. The same is true of other uses of *"vous/you"* in the text.

[55] See *Revelations 5:5*.

[56] See *Revelations 5:1*.

[57] *Luke 10:18*.

[58] See *Luke 10:19*.

[59] The remainder of this section is *Psalm 24*.

Lord Almighty, Lord Conqueror in Battles. Princes, open your Gates. Raise up the Eternal Gates. Who is this King of Glory, the Lord Almighty? This Lord is the King of Glory. Gloria Patri[60] *&c."*

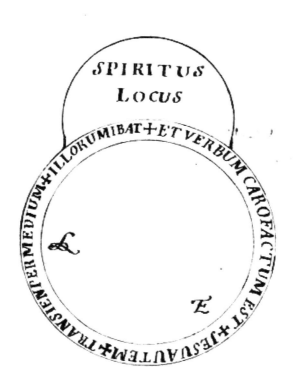

61

(188) The Circle represented below can be used for the four following Conjurations, which can be recited every day and at any hour. And if you wish to speak to just one Spirit, only one shall be called from them and that is in accordance with the will of the Operator.

---

[60] Latin: *"Glory to the father".* In full: *"Gloria Patri, et Filio, et Spiritui Sancto, Sicut erat in principio, et nunc, et semper, et in saecula saeculorum. Amen."* The English of this reads *"Glory to the Father, and to the Son, and to the Holy Spirit, As it was in the beginning, also now, and always, and to the ages of ages. Amen."*

[61] The upper partial circle contains the Latin words *"Spiritus Locus"* – *"Spirit Place"*, and the circles contain the Latin *"Iesus autem transiens per medium illorum ibat + et verbum caro factum est"* meaning *"But Jesus, passing through the midst of them, went His way and the word was made flesh"*, these quotes coming from *Luke 4:30, John 1:14.*

62

There are certain observations to be made concerning the Four Kings and their Conjurations, for this is what has been given in the *Grimoire of Pope Honorius*. The King of the East is the powerful *Magoa*. But according to the manuscript or *"the dark manuscript"*, he is *Payemon*. And according to J.B.[63] and Agrippa,[64] The Four Principle Spirits, who control or dwell in the Four Elemental Quarters are as follows: in the East, the Spirit is called **ORIENS**; the Spirit of the West is called *Payemon*; the Spirit of the South is called *Œgim* and the Spirit of the Northern Quarter is called *Amaymon*. Here follows the

---

[62] The outer circle contains the French phrase *"Delivrez nous Notre Seigneur Par le Signe de la Croix de nos Ennemis"* meaning *"Deliver us our Lord by the sign of the Cross from our enemies"*, and the square contains two Hebrew divine names separated by the French word *delivrez* - *"Tetragrammaton, Delivrez [Deliver], Saday"*

[63] Jacques Bellot.

[64] Heinrich Cornelius Agrippa, (1486-1535), the famous German magician best known for the classic *Three Books of Occult Philosophy*.

Four Conjurations for the Four Kings of the Four Quarters of the World.

There then follow the Conjurations for various Spirits according to the Days of the Week, namely: Monday to **LUCIFER**, Tuesday to **NAMBROTH**, Wednesday to **ASTAROTH**, Thursday to **ACHAM**, Friday to **BECHET**, Saturday to **NABAM** and Sunday to **AQUIEL**. (189)

CONJURATION OF THE KING OF THE EAST

"I conjure thee and invoke thee, Oh mighty N.[65] *King of the East, by my Holy Work, by all the names of the Divinity, by the name of the Almighty, I command thee to obey me and to come or forthwith send me N. without retardation, Massniel, Asiel, Satiel, Arduel, Acorib and with no delay in order to respond to that, which I wish to know and do that, which I command or thou wilt come thyself in order to satisfy my desire. And if thou dost not do so, I shall thereby compel thee by all the Virtue and Power of God."*

CONJURATION OF THE KING OF THE WEST

*"**Oh King Bayemont!**[66] Most powerful, who reigneth in the Western Quarters, I call thee and invoke thee in the name of the Divinity; I command thee by the virtue of the Most High to forthwith send me before this Circle N. Passiel, Rosus with all the other Spirits, who are subject unto thee, that they may respond unto all that I shall request of them and if thou dost not do so, I shall torment thee, with the sword of divine fire, I shall increase thy suffering and shall burn thee."*

CONJURATION OF THE KING OF THE SOUTH

*"**Œgim!**[67] Great King of the South, I conjure thee and invoke thee by the Most High and Holy Names of God to act in accordance with your rank and by thy power to*

---

[65] As noted in the text, there appear different names for the King of the East. The 1760/1810 text gives the name as *'Magoa'* and the 1800 edition text gives the name *'Nagoa'*.

[66] The 1760/1810 and 1800 texts both spell the name *'Bayemon'*. The pronunciation for both names is however identical in French.

[67] The 1760/1810 and 1800 text spell the name *'Egym'*. There are other variants of the name, such as *'Egim'* and *'Egin'*. By and large, all these names would have a similar or identical pronunciation in spoken French /œ'gĩ/, which would account for the written variations.

come before this Circle or send me forthwith Fadal, Nastraché in order to respond and execute all my desires and if thou dost not do so, I shall compel thee by God Himself."

CONJURATION OF THE KING OF THE NORTH

"Oh thou Amaymon, King and Emperor of the Northern Quarters, I call invoke, exorcise and conjure thee by the Virtue and Power of the Creator and by the virtue of all virtues to immediately send me and without delay Madael, Laaval, Bamulahe,[68] Belem, Ramath with all the other Spirits, who are subject unto thee in a comely and human form. In whatever place that thou mayest be, come render honour that thou owest unto the True God and thy Creator. In the Name of the Father and of the Son and of the Holy Ghost, come, therefore, and be obedient before this Circle, with no peril to my body or soul. Come in a comely human and not in any terrible form. I implore thee to come forthwith and immediately. (190) By all the Divine Names, Sechiel, Barachiel, if thou dost not swiftly come, Balandir, suspensus,[69] iracundis,[70] origatiumgu,[71] Partus, olemdemis and Bantaris N. I exorcise thee, invoke and command thee most highly, by all the power of the Living God, by the True God, by the virtue of the Holy God and by the virtue of The One who spake and everything was made and by whose Holy Commandment all things were made, the Heavens, the Earth and that, which is in them. I implore thee by the Father, by the Son and by the Holy Ghost and by the Holy Trinity and by the God, to whom thou canst not resist, under whose Empire I shall make thee bow; I conjure thee by God the Father, by God the Son and by God the Holy Ghost and by the Mother of Jesus Christ, St Mary and Perpetual Virgin and by Her Holy Womb[72] and by her most sacred milk, upon which God the Son suckled; and by her most Holy Body and Soul and by all the body parts and members of this Virgin and by all the sufferings and by all the afflictions, labours and bitterness that she endured during her life; by all the sighs and Holy tears that she shed, while her dear son cried before his time of painful Passion on the Tree of the Cross; by all the Holy and Sacred things, which are offered and done and by all others on Earth, as it is in Heaven to the honour of OSJC[73] and of the blessèd Virgin Mary, his mother and by all that is celestial, by the Church Militant,[74] in honour of the Virgin

---

[68] 1760/1810 *"Bamulhae"*.

[69] Latin: *"hanging"*.

[70] Latin: *"by the anger"*.

[71] A divine, angelic name.

[72] Other texts state *"by her Sacred Heart"*.

[73] *"Our Saviour Jesus Christ"*: In French, the abbreviation is *"NSJC"* for Notre Sauveur Jésus Christ.

[74] *"L'Église militante, l'assemblée des fidèles sur la terre, par opposition à l'Église triomphante (les*

and of all the Saints and by the Holy Trinity and by all the other Mysteries and by the Sign of the Cross and by the most precious Blood and Water which flowed from the side of Jesus Christ and by his proclamation[75] and by the sweat which issued from all his body, when in the Garden of Olives[76] he said, "My Father, if it is possible, may these things pass me by, so that I may not drink of the Cup of Death"; by his Death and Passion and by his burial and by his glorious Resurrection, by his Ascension, by the Coming of the Holy Ghost, I adjure thee anew by the Crown of Thorns, which he bore upon his head, by the blood, which flowed from the wounds on his feet and hands, by the nails, with which he was nailed to the Tree of the Cross and by the Five Wounds, by the holy tears, which he shed and by all that he suffered willingly with great charity for our sakes; by the lungs, by the heart, by the liver, by the bowels and by all the limbs of OSJC; by the Judgement of the Quick and the Dead, by the Gospel words of OSJC, by his preachings, by his sayings, by all his miracles, by the child wrapped in a swaddling cloth, by the crying child, which the mother bore in her most pure and virginal womb, by the glorious Intercessions of the Virgin Mother of OSJC. (191) By all that is of God and of his Most Holy Mother, on Earth, as it is in Heaven, by the Holy Angels and Archangels and by all the Blessèd Ones, by the Holy Patriarchs and Prophets and by all the Blessèd and Holy Martyrs and Confessors, and by all the Holy Virgins and innocent widows and by all the Saints, both men and women and by the one sent from God, I conjure thee by the head of St John the Baptist, by the milk of St Catherine[77] and by all the Blessèd Ones."

---

saints, les bienheureux), et à l'Église souffrante (les âmes du purgatoire)". *"The Church Militant, the assembly of faithful upon the Earth, in opposition to the Church Triumphant (the saints, the blessèd ones) and The Church Suffering (souls in Purgatory)."* These terms are often used in the context of the doctrine of the Communion of Saints.

[75] Literally, *"annunciation"* see: *Luke 1:26* The Annunciation of the Blessèd Virgin Mary: the announcment by the Archangel Gabriel to Mary that she would become the Mother of the Son of God. It could be translated as *"his declatration while Jesus was on the cross"*, which would make better sense as we are talking about the Passion of Jesus Christ here and not the Announcement of the Angel Gabriel to Mary, his mother.

[76] Also known as Gethsemane.

[77] St Catherine was a noted saint from the 4th Century CE, who was born in Alexandria, She was born to a pagan father, but later converted to Christianity. She was to be executed on a spiked wheel after the Roman Emperor Maxentius failed to turn her back to paganism, but the wheel broke and she was consequently executed by beheading instead. It is said that angels carried her body to Mount Sinai, where a monastery was founded. A later medieval Cult developed centuries later after her body was purportedly found, with her hair still growing and a healing ointment exuding from her body.

CONJURATION OF THE KINGS OF THE SOUTH

"I conjure thee, N. rebellious Spirit of Air of the South by the Authority and Virtue of the Holy Names of God hereafter, to appear in a comely form before this Circle and obey me, N. who is a Creature of the Most High and Supreme Divinity Jesus of Nazareth +and I thereby conjure thee by his Nativity, by his Death and Passion and Resurrection, by the Virgin Mary ever Virginal, by the Authority of his Apostles and preachings, by their martyrs and celestial glories and I thereby conjure thee for the third and last time, by these general and ineffable names: **Tetragrammaton + Jeva + Jehova Agla + Shaday + Elohim + Sabaot + Saday + Sother + Emanuel + El + Theos +**. *Mayest thou appear without delay and with no deceit, without changing thy response unto me and obey me in all that I desire of thee. If not, I shall banish thee into the Abyss of Hell to abide there according to my will. Behold this Pentacle, which is the force and power of the Most High.* **Ya, He, Vau, Bet, Gimel, Lomet, Sabaot +"**

The characters represented below are those of the Spirit of Darkness, **LEVIATHANT**[78]

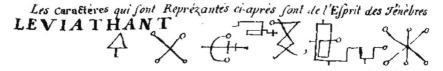

This Spirit is extremely formidable and he is a commander of twenty seven Legions. According to the report from Uverius, he has great abilities, such as being able to transmute metals, precious stones, properties of simple plants, herbs and animals and even treasures hidden in the bowels of the Earth. Calling him must be made in the direction of the Southern Quarter, at the hours for the Planets of Saturn, the Moon and Mars, in the Signs of the Fish or the Ram. His appearance is quite formidable and strikes fear, appearing in the many hideous guises of monsters and ferocious animals. In order to restrain him, you will need to perform a most powerful conjuration (192) and possess much courage, firmness and boldness, whilst actually being in the Circle itself, which is for your own defence and protection. He speaks

---

[78] A Leviathan is a sea-monster that is mentioned in the Bible, most notably in the *Book of Job*, chapter 41. It is also the name of one of the three more prominent fallen angels in Christian demonology, who is the gatekeeper of Hell and also one of the seven princes of Hell.

like a clap of thunder, he carries the Witches, who have made a pact with him to their Sabbats, he bestows powders and unguents, he bestows familiar Spirits, which are useful to you for all manner of things. Be wary of his ensnarements, for he seeks but to trick you in all things. He often speaks without making himself appear in order to better trap you in his snares and he promises you many things.

Following the report from the same Uverius, below are the characters of the Spirit, who is called **BERITH**[79]

Suivant le Raport du même **Uverius** *, Voici-ci-après les caractères de l'Esprit qui se nomme* **BERITH**

Here are the qualities and virtues, which he declares to be for this Spirit. He says that *Bérith* is a Spirit, who is fairly docile, who only replies to the person, who questions him. He appears at eleven o'clock in the evening, the Moon being new and waxing and in the Sign of the Ram, the Bull or the Lion. His characters must be made on goatskin. He has great virtues and great powers, for he commands many Legions of Spirits. He is a Spirit of the North and he resides in Watery Places. He has great power over the waters, fish and over all manner of aquatic animals, herbs, rocks, metals and shipping.

The most appropriate days for him are Tuesday, Thursday and Saturday.

His Invocation and Conjuration are always performed during the Nocturnal Hours.

Here is his Invocation and Conjuration, which is simple and brief in manner.

"I conjure thee, Bérith, by the Most Holy Trinity, Father ✝ Son and Holy ✝ Spirit, Sanctus, Sanctus, Dominus Deus Sabahot[80] *✝ Elohim Jeova ✝"*

He will appear to you on the third time that you recite this Conjuration in the guise of a King, richly clothed with great splendour and with majestic grandeur. And he speaks in a loud voice.

---

[79] Bérith is described as a messenger of Paymon as King of the West in Sloane 3824 (1649). He previously appears as a Spirit of Earth in the German work *Magia Naturalis et Innaturalis* (1505).
[80] Latin: *"Holy, Holy, Lord God Sabaoth"* (the last word clearly being a corruption of this divine name)

The characters that follow are of Prince **BELZEBUTH**.[81]

(193)

CONJURATION and Evocation to BELZEBUT

"*BELZEBUT, Lucifer, Madilon, Asohym, Osaroy, Thers, Amedo, Segrael, Praredon, Adricahorom, Martir, Timot, Lameron, Phorsy, Metonte, Prumosy, Dumaso, Divisa, Alphroys, Fubentronty. Venite*[82] *Belzebut Amen.*"

There are three principal Spirits or Intelligences, which are under the Dominion of Belzebut, namely, Egalierap, Tarchimache and Fleruty.

Here are their characters

 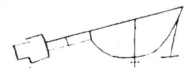

---

[81] A variant spelling of *"Beelzebub"*.
[82] Latin: *"come"*.

CONJURATIONS FOR THE SEVEN DAYS OF THE WEEK
FOR MONDAY TO LUCIFER

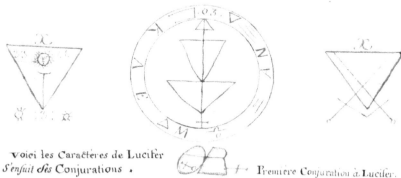

Voici les Caractères de Lucifer S'enfuit des Conjurations .

Première Conjuration à Lucifer.

Here are the characters of Lucifer:

which are followed by his Conjurations.

FIRST CONJURATION TO LUCIFER

'LUCIFER + *Oviar* + *Chameron* + *Aliscor* + *Mandusin* + *Premy* + *Oriel* + *Mayrdrus* + *Osmony* + *Eparine* + *Sont* + *Estio* + *Dumoson* + *Donoar* + *Casmiel* + *Hagras* + *Fabbrom* + *Honsi* + *Sordinot* + *Pratham* + *Venité* + *Lucifer* + *Amen* +''

The two intelligences that are subject to them are **SATHAN**[83] and **ACHIA**.

Note that I have not found the characters for these two Intelligences, which should not hinder the evocation. But I have found the character for **SATANACHI**, which is under **SIRACHI** and is related to Lucifer. See Page 148 in the *Key of Psalms*.[84] It would be wise to refer to Philosophy for more about the Intelligences. (194)

---

[83] A variant spelling for *"Satan"*.

[84] This is probably *Clef des Psaumes*, L'Abbé Foinard, Paris, 1740

The operation for Lucifer is often performed from eleven o'clock until twelve and from three until four. You will need some charcoal or some consecrated chalk in order to construct the circle, unless better advised, to form each Circle... around which you will write the following: *"I forbid thee, Lucifer, in the Name of the Most Holy Trinity, to enter into this Circle"*

You should have a mouse ready to give to him for when you banish him. The Operator must have some Holy Water and should be clothed in a surplice[85] or an alb[86] and a stole[87] in order to begin the Conjuration with a cheerful disposition and pronounce his commandments fiercely and brusquely, as a Master would speak to his servant, with all manner of threats, using the following terms: *"Satam, Rantam, Pallantre, Lutais, Cricacoeur, Scircigreur, I summon thee most humbly to render unto me &c..."*

It is better to recite the First Conjuration above, *"Lucifer + Oviar &c..."*

SECOND CONJURATION TO LUCIFER

"I conjure thee, Lucifer, by the Living God, by the True God, by the Holy God, by the God, who spake and all things were made; He uttered a commandment and all things were made and created. I conjure thee by the **ineffable Name of God, ON, Alpha and Omega, Eloy, Eloym, Ya, Saday, Lux, the Mugiens, Rex, Salus, Adonay, Emmanuel, Messias** *and I adjure thee, conjure and exorcise thee by the Names, which are declared by the letters V.G.X. and by the Names* **Jeova, Sol, Agla, Rassosoris, Oriston, Ophitue, Phaton, Ipretu, Ogia, Speraton, Imagnon, Amul, Penaton, ON, Perchiram, Tiros, Rubiphaton, Simulaton, Perpi, Klarimum, Tremendum, Meraye** *and by the Most High Ineffable Names of God,* **Gali, Enga, El, Abdanum, Ingodum, Obu, Englabis**, *to come or to send me N. in a comely and human form and with no unsightliness, to reply with complete truth all that I shall ask of him, having no power to harm me, neither in body, nor in soul, nor any person whatsoever."*

---

[85] The ceremonial white tunic that fits over the robe of the Priest.

[86] A ceremonial white robe coming down to the feet used by a Priest. This is similar to a cassock, which is usually black.

[87] A Stole is the ceremonial band of cloth worn across the Priest's shoulder and hangs down his body.

FOR TUESDAY TO NAMBROTH[88]

APOLONIUS & THANIUS[89] say that he is a most formidable Spirit, who has many Legions of Spirits under him. He governs Syria[90] and attends the Nocturnal Assemblies of the Lebanese. He appears in various forms, but most frequently as a satyr. He makes loud noises, with peals of thunder and flashes of lightning; he loves perfumes and appears on Saturday nights during the New Moon, when it is in the sign of the Lion, as you may see in his character. He bestows familiar Spirits and he is the (195) Guardian of Riches and Treasures hidden in the Earth. But a great and most potent Conjuration is necessary to make him obey. This is why it is necessary to be most wary of him, for he is most wicked and terrible when he is approached, as RAZIEL strongly suggests. He keeps to caverns and inhospitable places on mountains and amongst the ferocious and cruel beasts of Libya and he is often found on Mount Hetna[91]... His character must be made on purified lead, during a New Moon, when She is in the Sign of the Lion. This lead metal must be made into a thin plate.

---

[88] The 1760/1810 text gives the name *Frimost*. He is named in the *Grimoire Verum* as a demon who can control the minds of women and girls.

[89] Probably a corruption of Apollonius of Tyana. The pseudepigraphical *Nuctameron of Apollonius of Tyana* established a link between Apollonius and demons, which this may be playing on, as Nambroth is not mentioned in the text.

[90] In Classical terms, Ancient Syria (or Greater Syria) more or less covers the area that we these days call *'The Levant'*, which covers modern-day Syria, as well as the Lebanon and Israel along with the Palestinian Territories and includes parts of Jordan, Iraq and Turkey.

[91] This is the Greek transliteration for Etna, the volcano found on the Italian Island of Sicily. The first letter has a *'breathed'* (or aspirated) diacritic in Greek, which is why it is written as *"Hetna"* in the text.

Figure of the Character of NAMBROTH

This operation is performed at night, from nine o'clock until ten o'clock. You should give him the first stone that you find. This is in order to be received with dignity and honour. You will thence proceed as in the manner for Monday. You will make a Circle, around which will be written: *"Obey me, Nambroth, Obey me Nambroth, Obey me Nambroth."*

CONJURATION

"I conjure thee, Nambroth and command thee by all the Names wherewith thou mayest be constrained and bound. I exorcise thee Nambroth by thy Name, by the virtue of all the Spirits, by all the Characters, by the Pentacle of Solomon, by the Jewish, Greek and Chaldean Conjurations and by confusion and malediction and I shall redouble thy sufferings and torments from day to day for evermore, if thou dost not come forthwith to fulfil my will and submit to all that I shall command of thee, having no power to harm me, either in body, in soul, or harm those in my Company."

WEDNESDAY FOR ASTAROTH[92]

This operation is done between ten o'clock and eleven o'clock; it is in order to acquire the good graces of the Emperor, of Kings or of other powerful Sovereigns &c. In order to execute this operation, you should be clothed in white linen (196) and have some consecrated chalk, with which

---

[92] Astaroth, a male demon, was originally a Canaanite goddess, known as Ashtoreth.

you will form the Circle and the names, as is shown below, within which you will place yourself in order to perform the Conjurations. While the perfumes burn, you will say that, which follows:

"*Conjuro te* **ASTAROTH**. *Per sanguinem Jesum Christum ✝ Apud Aparitio ad te ✝ Venisti quid venire and veni cumplaceat and crime ✝*"[93]

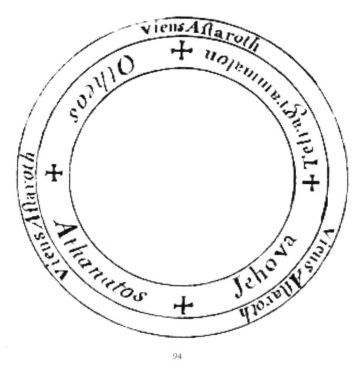

94

As has been mentioned in several places, you should make the circles and write what needs to be written with charcoal or with consecrated chalk. You can also make them on strips of paper stitched or pasted together, so that you can double the size of the canvas, so that it will be easier to write what needs to be written and you should write this with the pen and the ink of the Art and everything should be arranged according to the Art. And when the Circle has been made sufficiently large, following the model as given above. You will enter into it, having placed it in a suitable place and

---

[93] Latin: *"I conjure thee, Astaroth, by the blood of Jesus Christ ✝ amongst thy servants ✝ that thou mayest come & come that it may be pleasing & by the charge."*
[94] The outer circle contains the French phrase *"Viens Astaroth"* meaning *"Come Astaroth"*, and the inner circle contains the divine names *"Otheos"*, *"Athanatos"*, *"Tetragrammaton"* and *"Jehova"*.

location, then you will say the following Conjuration:

CONJURATION

"*I conjure thee Astaroth, Wicked Spirit, by the words and virtues of God and by the Almighty God and by Jesus Christ of Nazareth, unto whom all Dæmons are subject, who was conceived of the Virgin Mary, through the Mystery of the Angel Gabriel. I conjure thee anew in the Name of the Father and of the Son and of the Holy Ghost; in the Name of the glorious Virgin Mary and of the Most Holy Trinity, in whose honour all the Archangels, Thrones, Dominions, Powers, Patriarchs, Prophets, Apostles and Evangelists sing without end, "Holy, Holy, Holy, the Lord God of Hosts, who was, who is and who shall come as a river of blazing fire. Disregard not my commandments and (197) refuse not to come. I command thee by the one who will come in fire, to judge the Quick and the Dead, unto whom all honour, praise and glory is due. Come promptly, therefore, and obey my will; come, therefore, and give honour unto the True God, unto the Living God and unto all his Works and do not thou fail to obey me and give honour unto the Holy Ghost in whose Name I command thee.*"

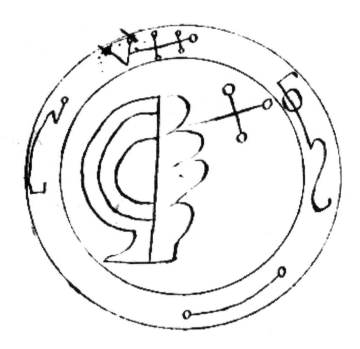

The Circle once made as has been shown here and having followed the instructions that have been given to you above and having at hand the character referred to below, you will then enter into the said Circle and you will recite the Conjuration below and you will add the following, having already recited the *"Canticle of the Three Children in the Furnace"*,[95] *"The Grace"*[96] &c and Ps148 *"Laudate"* &c. beforehand and three times in succession.

CONJURATIONS

"I, N., do conjure thee Spirit N. in the Name of the Great Living God, who hath made the Heavens and the Earth and all that is contained therein, by the Virtue of the Holy Ghost and of the Holy Name of J.C., the dearest Son of the Most High, who suffered Death and Passion and by the precious Love of the Holy Ghost and perfect Trinity, that thou mayest appear unto me in a pleasant form and without noise. I conjure thee in the Name of the Great Living God."

"ADONAY + Tetragrammaton + Adonay + Jehova Otheos Athanatos Adonay Jehova Otheos Athanatos Adonay Jehova Otheos Athanatos Tettragrammaton Aluciat Adonay Ischiros Athanatos Saday, Saday, Saday, Adonay + Saday, Tetragrammaton Saday, Jehova, Adonay, Elohy, Elohy, Agla, Elohy, Agla, Adonay, Adonay, ADONAY +"

Having said these Conjurations three times in succession, you will immediately hear a concert (198) of all manner of music by various instruments, but there is no need to be alarmed by any of what you hear or see. Moreover, you will see many spectres that may cause you to be fearful, but above all, do not move and do not leave the Circle for any reason, until these visions have disappeared and if they remain too long, you should say the following words three times:

"Otheos, Otheos, Otheos, Athanatos, Ischiros, Athanatos, Adonay, Adonay, Adonay, Jehova, Tetragrammaton +"

---

[95] This is a passage that occurs in the Bible in *Daniel 3:23*. It can only be found in the Catholic and Eastern Orthodox versions of the Bible and it has been omitted from Protestant Bibles. It is also found in the *Septuagint*. It refers to the penitential Prayer of Azariah, while the three youths Sidrach, Misach and Abdenago were within the furnace. It is included in the Deuterocanonical (or Apocryphal) Books of the Bible, and is often inserted into the third chapter in the *Book of Daniel*.

[96] The *Benedicite* is normally the *'Grace'* said before meals but here it refers to the canticle that is found in the Church of England *Book of Prayer*.

As soon as you have finished these words, they should disappear unless the Spirits seek only to cause fear. But have courage, for they are but illusions. When all these phantoms have disappeared, the Spirit will appear to you and then you can ask him what you desire and being satisfied, you should discharge him and thank him with the words of the Discharge on Page 131, whilst showing him the Pentacle.[97]

OBSERVATIONS NECESSARY FOR THE CONJURATIONS OF THE SPIRITS AS WELL AS THE DISCHARGES, WHILST IN THE CIRCLE.

Be warned that when you perform the Conjurations whilst in the Circle, you should not leave the Circle at all, no matter what you hear, no matter what noises there be and if they bring you what you asked of them, you should banish them with the following Discharge.

DISCHARGE OF THE SPIRITS, WHILST IN THE CIRCLE

"In the Name + of the Father + and of the Son + and of the Holy Ghost, go in peace to your retreats and may Peace reign between us and be ye ever prepared to come as soon as I shall call you."

It should be noted here as something that is most important, that these Conjurations for calling Spirits and the contract or agreement that you make with them, should be written on Virgin Parchment (prepared according to the Art) made from the skin of a suckling lamb and you should recite or pronounce the *Gospel of St John* over it, as has been reported below, with their Pentacles. They should be blessed and aspersed by a Priest, if possible, otherwise, the Spirits will not appear at all and they will be of no use to you, other than to disturb and annoy you in various ways.

It should also be noted that the character for each Spirit should be made or written with the blood of a young chicken that has not been castrated. In principle, when you wish to conjure and evoke any Prince or Duke it should

---

[97] P.131 reads: *"Here is your sentence, which forbids you from being rebellious to our will and which orders you to return to your dwelling places. May Peace be between us and be ready to return every time that I call you to do my will"*

always be with Virgin Parchment, as has been said, while reciting the *Gospel of St. John* over the said Parchment, as has been stated above. (199)

As is noted here below the Character, you should recite *"The Canticle of the 3 Children in the Furnace"* and *Psalm 148* 3 times, it is also wise to add it to the Oration below and add 5 *Pater* and 5 *Ave* &c.

"In Nomine Jesus omne flectatur Cœlestium Terrestrium & Infernorum & omnia lingua confiteatur quia Dominum noster Jesus Christus. In gloria Dei Patris ✝ & Filii ✝ & Spiritus Sancti ✝ Amen."[98]

Having thus recited all that has been mentioned for the preparation of the Work, you will immediately enter into the Circle, taking some roots from the Periwinkle flower, some Fern or Vervain with you, or even some of all three, if this is possible for you.

Then you will be able to do your Summoning Conjuration of the Spirits and you will witness how it takes effect. But above all, be chaste and pure both in sex as well as pure from other pollutants[99] for at least 3 days and you may be assured to have a complete satisfaction in all that you desire.

FOR THURSDAY TO ACHAM[100]

This operation is done at night from 3 o'clock until 4 o'clock, during which you conjure him and he will appear in the form of a King. You should give him a piece of bread in order for him to speak. This is in order to make him happy and it is also for treasures. You should write: *"By the Holy God. By the Holy God. By the Holy God"* around the Circle or write *"Adonay nasim pin 7.7. H M A."* in another Circle within in the first Circle.

---

[98] The prayer has been corrupted and should read *"omne genu flectatur"*. *"In nomine Jesu omne genu flectatur, coelestium, terrestrium, et infernorum: et omnis lingua confiteatur, quia Dominus Jesus Christus in gloria est Dei Patris. * Domine Dominus noster: quam admirabile est nomen tuum in universa terra!"*
*"In the Name of Jesus let every knee bow, of those that are in heaven, on earth, and under the earth: and let every tongue confess that the Lord Jesus Christ is in the glory of God the Father. * O Lord our Lord: how admirable is Thy Name in the whole earth!"* This is a Liturgical Introit, which is the first part of the Eucharist in Orthodox Christianity.
[99] E.g. tobacco and alcohol.
[100] Some of the texts give the name *Silcharde*, a ruling demon that can be only summoned on Thursday.

CONJURATION

"*I conjure thee, **ACHAM**, by the image and likeness of Jesus Christ Our Lord, whose death and Passion have redeemed mankind, who wisheth that by his Providence, that thou mayest appear here forthwith. I command thee by all the Kingdoms of God. Act, I adjure and constrain thee by his Holy Name, by The One, who walked upon the Asp, who crushed the Lion and the Dragon. Obey me and do my commandments with having no power to harm me, either in body, or in soul, or to anyone whomsoever.*"

FOR FRIDAY TO BECHET[101]

This operation is done only at night, that is to say, from eleven o'clock until midnight. You should give him a nut and you should write the following in the Circle for him:

"*Come Bechet! Come Bechet!*" (200)

CONJURATION

"*I conjure thee, **BECHET** and compel thee to come to me. I conjure thee anew by the Most Holy Names of God; **Eloy, Adonay, Agla, Samalabactani**, which are written in Hebrew, Greek and Latin; by all the sacraments, by all the Names written in this **BOOK** and by The One, who drove thee from the Highest Heaven, I conjure thee and command thee by the virtue of the Most Holy Trinity and by the Most Holy Eucharist, who hath redeemed men from their sins, that without delay to come, carry out and complete all my commandments with no injury either to my body, or to my soul, neither harming my Book, nor to those that are present here with me.*"

FOR SATURDAY TO NABAM[102]

This operation is done at night from eleven o'clock until midnight and as soon as he appears, you should give him some burnt bread. Ask him anything that pleases you and he will obey you on the spot. Write in his Circle "*Do not enter, Nabam, Do not enter, Nabam. Do not enter, Nabam*"

---

[101] The 1760/1810 text gives the name *Béchard*, a ruling demon that can be only summoned on Friday.
[102] The 1760/1810 text gives the name *Guland*, a demon that can be only summoned on Saturday.

CONJURATION

"I conjure thee, **NABAM***, in the Name of Sathan, in the Name of Belzébuth, in the Name of Astaroth and in the Name of all the other Spirits to come unto me. Come, then, unto me in the Name of Sathan and of all the other Dæmons. Come, then, unto me when I command thee in the Name of the Most Holy Trinity. Come without causing me ill, without injury, to my soul or to my body, without harming my* **BOOKS***, nor anything that I make use thereof. I command thee to come without delay, or send thou me another Spirit, which hath the same power as thyself, who shall carry out my commandments and may he be subject to my will, may the one that thou wilt send to me, if thou dost not come thyself, not leave without my consent and may he accomplish my will."*

FOR SUNDAY TO AQUIEL[103]

This operation is performed at night from midnight until one o'clock. He will ask you for a hair from your head but you should give him a hair from a fox. He should take this. This is for finding and transporting all the treasures that you desire. Write in his Circle: *"Tetragrammaton x3 Ismael, Adonay, Ilma"*. And in a second Circle: *"Come Aquiel! Come Aquiel! Come Aquiel!"*

CONJURATION (201)

"I conjure thee, Aquiel, by all the Names that are written in this Book, without delay and promptly to be present, ready to obey me. Or send thou a Spirit unto me, who shall bring me a stone, with which, when I shall carry it, I shall not be seen by any person, however he may be. And I conjure thee to subject thyself to the One that thou wilt send me, or to those, whom thou wilt send to me in order to do and accomplish my will and all that I command without harm to myself, nor to anyone whomsoever, so that thou knowest that, which I want."

---

[103] The 1760/1810 text gives the name *Surgat.* a demon that can be only summoned on Sunday.

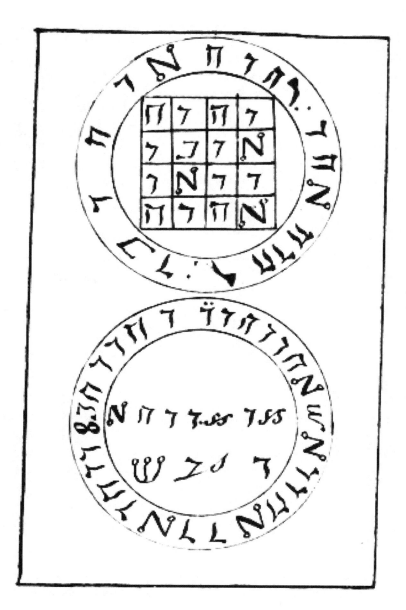

104

---

[104] The top figure appears to be a corrupted version of the first Pentacle of Saturn from the *Key of Solomon*, for striking terror into spirits to make them obey. The square contains corrupted forms of the divine names Jehovah (IHVH), Adonai

A MOST POWERFUL CONJURATION FOR ANY DAY AND ANY HOUR, DAY AND NIGHT, FOR TREASURES HIDDEN BY MEN AS WELL AS SPIRITS, TO HAVE THEM OR HAVE THEM TRANSPORTED.

"I command you, Oh Dæmons, who dwell in these places, or in whatever part of the World that ye may be and by whatever power hath been given unto you by God and by the Holy Angels over this very place and by the powerful Principalities of the Abysses of Hell and by all your brethren, Dæmons both general as well as particular of whatever order that ye may be, dwelling in the East, as well as the West, South and North and on any side of the Earth; by the power of God, the Father, by the wisdom of God the Son, by the virtue of the Holy Ghost and by the authority, which (202) *O.L.J.C. the only Son of the Almighty and Creator hath given me, who hath created us and all Creatures from nothing, who maketh you to lose your power to guard, reside and abide in this place, by whom I compel and command you, whether you like it or not, without deceit or trickery, that ye declare your names unto me and that ye bestow me with the quiet power over this place and of whatever legion ye may be and in whatever part of the World in which ye may dwell therein, by the Most Holy Trinity and by the mysteries of the Most Holy Blessèd Virgin and by all the Saints, I stir you up, Spirits all, who dwell in this place and I send you to the deepest of the Infernal Abysses. Thus, depart, all wicked and damned Spirits unto the eternal Fire, which is prepared for you and for all your companions if ye are rebellious towards me and are disobedient. I conjure you by the same authority. I exhort and call you. I compel and command you by all the powers of your Superior Dæmons, to come, obey and respond positively to that, which I order you in the name of J.C. that if they or ye do not obey promptly and without delay, in brief, I shall increase your sufferings in Hell for a thousand years. I compel you, therefore, to appear here in a comely human form, by all the **Most Holy Names of God. Hain, Lon, Hilay, Sabaoth, Helim, Radiaha, Ledieha, Adonay, Jeova, Ya, Tetragrammaton, Saday, Messias, Agios, Isehiros, Emmanuel, Agla, Jesus**, who is **Alpha and Omega**, the Beginning and the End, that ye be in the deepest of Abysses, in the fire justly established, so that ye may have no power, to once more dwell, reside or abide in this place and I ask what ye will do, by the virtue of the aforesaid Names and may the Angel St Michael send you to the deepest Infernal Chasm, in the Name of the Father and of the Son and of the Holy Ghost, so mote it be."*

*"I conjure thee, Acham, or whoever thou mayest be, by the **Most Holy Names***

(ADNI), Yiai (IIAI) and Eheieh (AHIH). The corrupted outer Hebrew is thus probably therefore *Psalm 72:9*; *"The Ethiopians shall kneel before him, his enemies shall lick the dust"*.

of God, by Malhame, Jac, May, Mabron, Jacob, Dasmedias, Eloy, Aterestin, Janastardy, Finis, Agios, Ischiros, Otheos, Atanatos, Agla, Jeova, Homausion, Aja, Messies, Sother, Christus, Vincit, Christus regnat, Christus imperat, increatur Spiritus Sanctum."[105]

"I conjure thee, Cassiel,[106] *or whomsoever thou mayest be, by all the aforesaid Names with power and exorcising thee thereof; I advise thee anew by the other aforementioned Names of the Creator Most Great, which are or shall hereafter be communicated to thee, so that thou mayest hear my words forthwith and right now and mayest thou observe them inviolably as sentences of the Last Day trembling with judgement, to which thou must obey me inviolably. And think thou not to reject me because I am a great sinner but know that thou repulsest the commandments of the God Most High. Knowest thou not, that thou losest thy strengths before thy Creator and ours? It is why thou shouldst think of that, which thou refusest me, as well (203) as that which thou promisest and swear by this Final Day, trembling with Judgement and by He, who hath created all with one sole word, whom all creatures obey. P. Per sedem Baldacy et per gratiam et diligentem tuam habuisti ab eo hac nalatimanamilam,*[107] *so that I may ask thee."*

THE HOLY GOSPEL ACCORDING TO ST JOHN

"N.N.N. I do invoke you, N. and compel you by the most powerful virtue of Jesus of Nazareth to make yourself appear presently in a fair, human figure and this is in order to reply to my question."

BEGINNING OF THE HOLY GOSPEL ACCORDING TO ST JOHN

"In the + Beginning was the Word and the Word was with God and the Word was God; it was from the Beginning in God. All things have been made by him and nothing that hath been made, was made without him. In him was Life and the Life was the light

---

[105] Latin: *"He [Christ] conquereth, Christ reigneth, Christ ruleth, begotten by the Holy Spirit".*
[106] The inclusion of the Saturnian archangel here seems curious, but this conjuration is repeated subsequently in other works.
[107] Latin: *"By the throne of Baldacy, & by thy grace, & conscientiousness hast thou received nalatimanamilam [the hidden that became manifest after] from this."* Nalatimanamilam is a corruption of one or more words combined, of unknown meaning. Tentatively, it could be broken down into several parts which give a coherent meaning: lati[to] - hidden/concealed, manam - became manifest, ilam – after, giving the suggested meaning included in the previous sentence.

N³.N³.N³. of men. And the light shineth *N³.N³.N³.* in the darkness and the *N³.N³.N³.* darkness comprehended it not. There was a man sent from God, who was called John. He came to give witness to the Light *N³.N³.N³.* so that through him all would believe. He was not the Light *N³.N³.N³.* but he came to bear witness to the one who was the Light *N³.N³.N³.*. That was the true Light that lighteth *N³.N³.N³.* all men *N³.N³.N³.* coming into this World. He was in the World and the World was made by him and the World knew him not. He had come unto his own and his own received him not, but to all those, who did receive him, he gave the power to be made into Children of God, even to those who believe in his Name, who were not born of Blood, nor of desires of the flesh, nor of the will of mankind, but of God himself. And the Word became Flesh *N³.N³.N³.* and he dwelt amongst us, full of grace and of truth and we have seen his glory, which is the glory of the Only Son of God. R; Render grace unto God *N³.N³.N³..*"

Note that at each place where there are three N³.N³.N³., thus represented, it is there that you have to name nine times the name of the one that you wish to make come and in the place where a Cross is marked, you should also name the name nine times. (204)

PENTACLE OF THE GOSPEL OF ST JOHN[108]

---

[108] This phrase is missing the word '*signio*' (sign or seal), as it usually reads "*In hoc signio vinces*", so it would have read "*In hoc signio vinces Adonay*", or "*Conquer in this name of Adonay*".

Here are the three small PENTACLES of SOLOMON

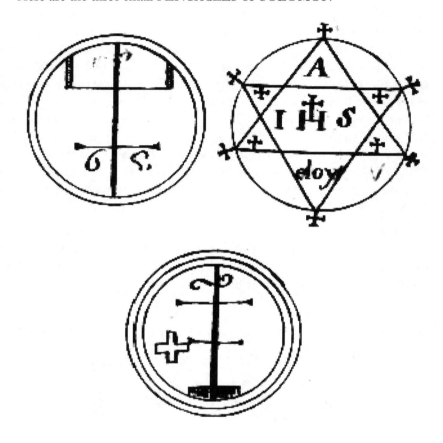

ADDITIONAL TEXTS

EDITORS' NOTES

We viewed a number of other versions of the *Veritable Grimoire of Pope Honorius*, all with different publishing dates, in addition to the Wellcome 4666 manuscript that forms the basis of this current work. To provide as thorough an overview as possible, we have detailed all the material found in these different editions, both that held in common and also the unique material.

Joseph H Peterson, who kindly supplied and allowed us to use the additional copies of the texts that he personally transcribed from original manuscripts, noted in 1999 that the 1760 [1810?] edition of the *Grimoire of Pope Honorius* was stolen from the British Library in 1972. However, when it was subsequently returned by the British Police, it had certain pages missing, which obviously rendered it incomplete. The missing pages were replaced by extrapolating the missing pages from a second intact 1800 edition. However, with the exception of a few minor variations, in particular the names of certain Intelligences and the order of listing for the various Collections of Secrets, these two editions are to all intents and purposes identical and it can be assumed that the extrapolation should not affect the authenticity of the stolen manuscript. Indeed each version that we have perused has been slightly different to the next, although they all have a commonality, that being the instructional body of methodology, prayers, conjurations and invocations.

Wellcome MS4666 actually contains several books, the principle one being a version of *The Key of Solomon*, but which also includes this book's account of Pope Honorius' Grimoire, thought its version of the *Grimoire of Pope Honorius* is missing the appendices that are known collectively as the Collection of Secrets. These secrets are of the type found in Books of

Secrets, which are essentially simple formulae, charms and spells for love, health, wealth and protection. A similar type of collection may be found in our work *A Collection of Magical Secrets/A Treatise of Mixed Cabalah* (2009).

The reader will note that there are bracketed numbers e.g. (23) throughout the text. These refer to page numbers in the original manuscripts and books. Wherever possible we have included footnotes translating the phrases used in the images found in the various works for the convenience of the reader.

David Rankine & Paul Harry Barron

February 2013

TRANSLATOR'S NOTES

The earliest of the copies that we have inspected dates from 1670, published in Rome, translated into French from the Latin and entitled *"Le Grimore du Pape Honorius, avec un Recueil des plus grands secrets de l'ART MAGIQUE et des practiques S'OPPOSANT aux MALÉFICES – à Rome 1670"* (*The Grimoire of Pope Honorius, with a Collection of some most great secrets of the Art Magical and some practices for Opposing Curses*). There are two other editions dating from the early 1800's that are very similar to each other, as we have already noted above, and we would consider them perhaps almost identical, with but very minor differences, which mostly concern the names for certain Intelligences, the differences of which can be found annotated in the present text. It might be said that there are also certain subtle differences in some of the diagrams throughout the various texts, but we are of the opinion, upon close inspection, that these may be regarded as stylistic differences, based on the individual artistic license of the transcribers, rather than actual structural differences. However, it should be pointed out that there are some significant differences in the Core Text. The additional texts contain lengthy passages that include additional conjurations, prayers and ritual instructions that are not contained in Wellcome 4666. This extra material generally precedes *The Conjuration of the Book*, which is the very first statement that we encounter in the Wellcome 4666 text but the texts generally converge once we arrive at the *Conjuration of Dæmons*.

Paul Harry Barron

February 2013

ADDITIONAL MATERIAL
FROM PRINTED EDITIONS OF
THE GRIMOIRE OF POPE HONORIUS

FROM THE ROME 1760 EDITION:

Guard for Sheep, Explained on page 106

GRIMOIRE[109] OF POPE HONORIUS

WITH A COLLECTION OF SOME OF THE RAREST SECRETS

In Rome 1760[110]

---

[109] In the less complete edition, the word is spelled as *'Gremoire'*. Note that some images are included from the 1800 edition, which are either different to those found in the 1760 edition, or are not found in it. The decision was taken to include them for completion and inform the reader as they occur so that they are aware of the continuity of the different editions.

[110] The Sigil is slightly different to the Sigil in the original text. The French words around the edge say *"Obeissez a vos superieurs et leur soyez soumis parce qu'ils y prennent garde"*, which translates as *"Obey your leaders and submit to their authority, for they keep watch over you."* (*Hebrews 13:17*).

PLATE II

Figure 2

Black cock indicated in page 8

Figure 3

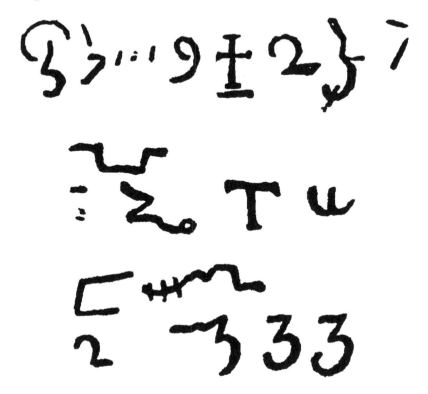

[Text to the left of each line: Line 1,[111] Line 2,[112] Line 3[113]]

---

[111] EL: (Latin) *pill que deum non vult deum non habet* – "whoever does not want God, does not have God".

[112] EL: (Latin) *qui vult deus est et christus* – "he who wants is God and Christ".

[113] EL: (Latin) *robur binarii est in negando teruario* – "the strength of the binary lies in negating the trinity (?)"*, followed by the number 666 which Levi seems to have added to the left of the *"2.333"* as their product with the Latin words *"hic est numerus antichristi"* – "here is the number of the antichrist".

PLATE III

Figure 4

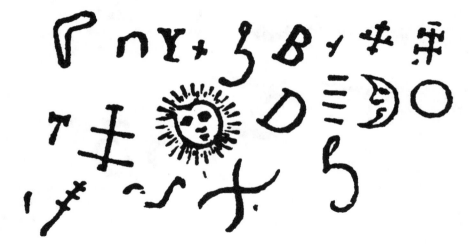

Figure 5 [114]

---

[114] EL: above the top line of the characters he added "*fatalitas*" (Latin) — "*by fate*"; next to the second line he added "*eclipsis solis et lunae*" (Latin) — "*of the eclipse of the sun and moon*"; under the bottom line he added "*regnum per serpentem*" (Latin) — "*the reign of the serpent*".

Figure 6

Agnus Dei q. t. p. m. m.[115] [116]

---

[115] This is clearly an abbreviation of the letters in the opening line of the *Agnus Dei* (Latin): "*Agnus Dei, qui tolis peccata mundi, miserere nobis*", which translates as "*Lamb of God, who take away sins of world, have mercy on us.*" Levi either did not make this connection, or tried to substitute something else. His notes give this explanation of the letters q.t.p.m.m. as "*quando tu potes moti moicre(?)*", which translates from Latin as "when you have the power to (*moicre?*) that which was moved"

[116] EL: "*credant quia absurdum*" (Latin) – "*they shall believe the absurd*". Underneath this EL added "*nomina et numeri blasphemia*" (Latin) – "*the names and numbers, blasphemy*".

83

PLATE IV

Figure 7

Figure 8

Figure 9[117]

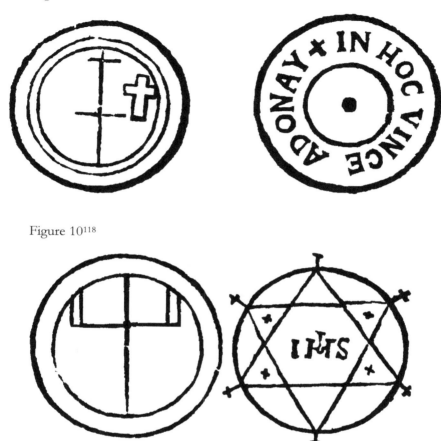

Figure 10[118]

NB: The figure for The Pentacle of Solomon, of which has been mentioned in this work, p. 21 and in *The Keys of Solomon* p. 66, [it] is found in Agrippa, p.16.

---

[117] This phrase is missing the word '*signio*' (sign or seal), as it usually reads "*In hoc signio vinces*", so it would have read "*In hoc signio vinces Adonay*", or "*Conquer in this name of Adonay*".

[118] The hexagon contains the letters IHS, the abbreviation for Jesus formed from the first three letters of his name in Greek (Iota, Eta, Sigma).

PLATE V

Figure 11[119]

---

[119] The circles contain the French *"Je te defends, Lucifer, au nom de la T.S.T. d'entrer dans ce cercle"*, meaning: *"I forbid thee, Lucifer, in the name of The Most Holy Trinity to enter into this Circle."*

Figure 12[120]

---

[120] The circles contain the Hebrew divine names Agla, Adonay, Jehova.

PLATE VI

Figure 13[121]

---

[121] The circles contain the French "*Viens Astaroth, viens Astaroth, viens Astaroth*", meaning "*Come Astaroth, come Astaroth, come Astaroth*". Note one of the spellings of Astaroth is miscopied with an r instead of an h at the end.

Figure 14[122]

---

[122] The circles contain the French *"Par le Dieu Saint, par le Dieu Saint, par le Dieu Saint"*, meaning *"By the Holy God, by the Holy God, by the Holy God."*

PLATE VII

Figure 15[123]

---

[123] The circles contain the French "*Viens Béchard, viens Béchard, viens Béchard*", meaning "*Come Béchard, come Béchard, come Béchard*".

Figure 16[124]

---

[124] The circles contain the French "*N'entre pas Guland, n'entre pas Guland, n'entre pas Guland*", meaning "*Do not enter Guland, do not enter Guland, do not enter Guland.*"

PLATE VIII

Figure 17[125]

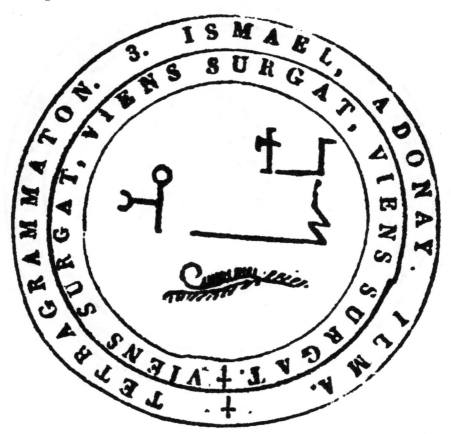

---

[125] The inner circles contain the French words *"Viens Surgat, viens Surgat, viens Surgat"*, meaning *"Come Surgat, come Surgat, come Surgat"*. The outer circles contain the divine names *"Tetragrammaton, Ismael, Adonay, Ilma"*.

92

Figure 18[126]

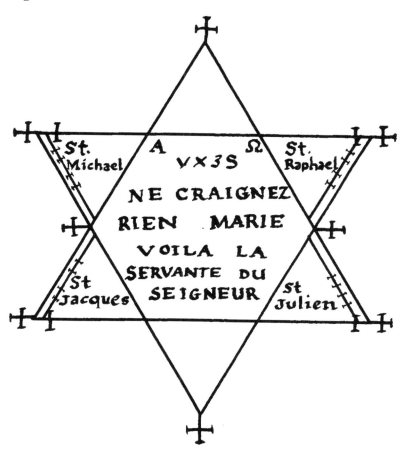

---

[126] The hexagon in the centre contains the Greek letters Alpha and Omega and the sequence VX3S, followed by the French words *"ne craignez rien Marie voila la servante du seigneur"*, meaning *'Fear nothing, Mary, behold God's handmaiden'*. The outer triangles contain the names of St Raphael, St Julien, St Jacques and St Michael.

Figure 19; Figure 20 [127]

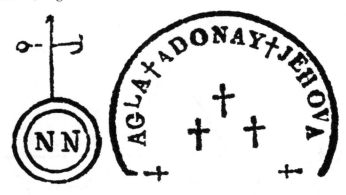

Figure 21[128]

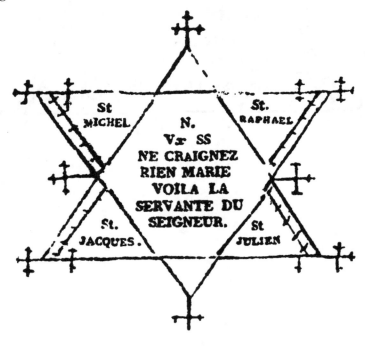

---

[127] The figure contains the Hebrew divine names "*Agla, Adonay, Jehova*".
[128] The hexagon in the centre contains the Greek letters Alpha and Omega and the sequence N. VXSS, followed by the French words "*ne craignez rien Marie voila la servante du seigneur*", meaning "*Fear nothing, Mary, behold God's handmaiden*". The outer triangles contain the names of St Raphael, St Julien, St Jacques and St Michael.

PLATE X

Figure 22[129]

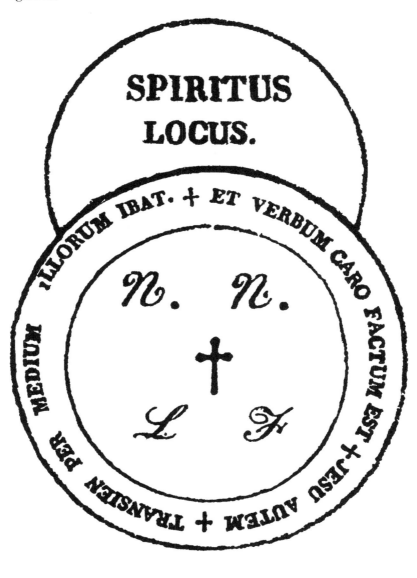

---

[129] The upper partial circle contains the Latin words "*Spiritus Locus*" – "*Spirit Place*", and the circles contain the Latin "*Iesus autem transiens per medium illorum ibat + et verbum caro factum est*" meaning "*But Jesus, passing through the midst of them, went His way and the word was made flesh*", these quotes coming from *Luke 4:30, John 1:14*.

Figure 23[130]

---

[130] The triangles contain the unknown words *"Satirne Gan Santalini"*.

PLATE XI

Figure 24

Saint Genevieve, Protectress of Flocks

(3)

CONSTITUTIONS
OF POPE HONORIUS THE GREAT

Where are found The Secret Conjurations which should be preformed against the Spirits of Darkness.

The Holy Apostolic See to which the Keys of the Kingdom of Heaven have been given by these words of J.C. to St Peter: *"I give thee the Keys of the Kingdom of Heaven"*, to thee sole power to command the Prince of Darkness and his Angels, who, as servants of their Master, owe him honour, glory and obedience, by the other words of J.C.: *"Thou wilt serve thy Lord"*; by the power of the Keys, the Head of the Church has been made Lord of the Hells.

For until today, The Supreme Pontiffs[131] alone have had the power (4) to call upon the Spirits and command them, but through his saintliness and pastoral concern, Honorius III has indeed desired to impart to his venerable brothers in J.C. the methods and the ability to call and command the Spirits, adding the conjurations, which need to be done for such cases. The complete contents are in the following Bull.

HONORIUS

Servant of the Servants of God. To all and every one of our venerable brothers of the Holy Roman Church the Cardinals, Archbishops, Bishops, Abbots; to all etc. And each one of our sons in J.C. the Priests, Deacons, Sub-deacons, Acolytes, Exorcists, Lectors,[132] Porters, Clerics, secular as well as regular, greeting and apostolic benediction. During the time that the Son of God, Saviour of the World, engendered before Time and born according to his humanity from the Race of the Seed of David, was living upon the Earth, whose Most Holy (5) Name is Jesus, before whom the Heavens, the

---

[131] i.e. all the Popes

[132] A *'lector'* in ecclesiastical terms is a member of the congregation, who has had a special rite said for them by the Roman Catholic Church so that they are institutionally allowed to read from the Scriptures during the Liturgy.

Earth and Hell must bend their knees, we have seen with what power he has commanded the Dæmons, whose power has been transmitted to St Peter; he has said, *"Upon this rock will I build my Church and the Gates of Hell shall not prevail against Her."* These words were addressed to St. Peter, as the Foundling Leader of the Church.[133]

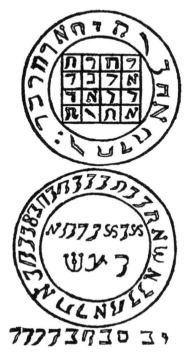

134

Therefore, through God's mercy, we have attained, despite what little

---

[133] The following illustration is included from the 1800 edition which also contains this material, as the 1760 edition does not have any images in this section.

[134] The lettering on these two seals is corrupted from the original Hebrew. They are found in *Key of Solomon* manuscripts, for Sunday under the Sun, see *The Veritable Key of Solomon*, Skinner & Rankine, 2008:115-6. They are also found previously in Agrippa's *De Occulta Philosophia* Book 3.11. Agrippa gives its source as Rabbi Hama's *Book of Speculation* (*Sefer Ha-Iyyun*). The first circle contains a 4x4 square with four divine names in it, IHVH (Yahveh), ADNI (Adonai), IIAI (Yiai), AHIH (Eheieh). This square is also found in the first pentacle of Saturn for striking terror into the spirits. The outer circles contain the Hebrew divine names AChD (Unity), IHVH, ALHIKV (Elohim), IHVH. The second (reverse) circle contains the Hebrew divine name ARARITA (Notariqon for a phrase meaning One is His beginning, One is His individuality, His permutation is One) in the centre with *Resh* underneath, with its expansion written around the edges *Achad Resh Achudohtoh Resh Yechidotoh Temurahtoh Resh*, the last *Resh* being written in the centre.

merit we possess, the Sovereign Apostolate,[135] and who, as the legitimate successor of St Peter, have in hand the Keys to the Kingdom of Heaven, wishing to impart the power to call and command, which has been reserved for us alone, and whose predecessors alone have enjoyed; desiring, as I say, to impart through divine inspiration, to our venerable brothers and dear sons in J.C., so that during the exorcism of the possessed, they may not be afraid (6) of horrible figures of these rebel Angels, whose sin has caused them to be hurled into the Abyss and so that they may neither lack instruction in that, which they need to do and to observe. And that in this way, those who have been redeemed by the blood of J.C. may not be afflicted by any curses nor possessed by any dæmon, we have enclosed within this Bull, the methods, with which to call them, which must be inviolably observed; and because it is agreed that those, who minister at the Altars should have authority over rebellious Spirits, we grant them all missives that we have, by virtue of the Holy Apostolic See, upon which we are exalted, and we order them, by our authority, to observe inviolably, that which follows, lest through shameful neglect of their character, they draw upon themselves the wrath of the Almighty.

The person named above, who would call the malign Spirits of Darkness should spend three days (7) fasting, make confession and approach the Holy Table. After these three days, on the next day at sunrise, he shall recite the Seven Gradual Psalms,[136] with the Litanies, and the Prayers, entirely upon his knees, neither should he drink any wine whatsoever on that day, nor eat any meat. He shall rise at midnight on the first Monday of the month and a Priest will say a Mass of the Holy Ghost.[137] After the consecration of the Host, taking it in his left hand, he will say the following prayer whilst upon his knees:

PRAYER

---

[135] The office and responsibilities of an Apostle in order to propagate the religious teachings of the Church.

[136] These may refer to the seven Penitential Psalms that were collated by Cassiodorus in the 6th Century CE and are chanted every day during Lent. They are Psalms 6, 31, 37, 50, 101, 129 & 142. The gradual Psalms, otherwise known as *Songs of Ascent*, were said to have been sung by pilgrims approaching Jerusalem, and are 15 in number, from Psalm 120-134. John Dee recommended using the Penitential Psalms, and they are also used in other Grimoires.

[137] This refers to the Red Mass in the Catholic Church. It is a Mass that is said to request the guidance of the Holy Spirit for people including judges, lawyers, law school professors, students, and government officials in the Catholic Church.

"My Lord Jesus Christ, son of the Living God, who for the Salvation of all mankind, you did suffer the torment of the Cross and who before being delivered unto your enemies, by a trait of your ineffable love, did you institute the Sacrament of your Body and who hath accorded to us the power, we miserable creatures, to daily commemorate thereof. Grant your (8) unworthy servant, who holdeth in his hands your living body, the force and power to make serviceable use of the power which hath been entrusted unto him against the horde of rebellious Spirits. It is you, who are their true Lord; if they tremble hearing your Holy Name, I shall invoke this Holy Name, saying J.C.! Jesus be thou my succour now and forever more. So mote it be!"

After sunrise, kill a black cockerel and take the first feather from its left wing, which you will preserve for use in due course. You must tear out the eyes, the tongue and the heart, which must be dried in the sun and which you will then reduce to a powder. At sunset, bury the rest of the cockerel in a secret place and set a cross upon the mound to the height of a palm leaf and with the thumb, at the Four Quarters, you will make the signs marked on the first line of figure 3, plate II.

He will drink no more wine on that (9) day; he will also abstain from eating any meat.

On Tuesday at dawn, he will say *The Mass of the Angels* and he will place the cockerel's feather upon the altar, which shall be cut with a new penknife and you will write on clean white paper with the blood of J.C. (consecrated wine) the figures represented in the same figure, second line.

He will write it on the altar and at the end of the Mass, he will fold this paper in a veil of violet silk and he will conceal it on the next day with the oblation of the Mass and a part of the consecrated Host.

On the eve of Thursday, he will rise at midnight and having sprinkled Holy Water around the room, he will light a church candle of yellow wax, which he will have prepared on Wednesday, which shall be pierced into the form of a Cross. And after it has been lit, he will say Psalm 77, "*Attendite, popule meus, legem meam* etc",[138] without saying the *Gloria Patri*.

He will begin *The Office of the Dead*[139] by "*Venite, exultemus Domino, etc*"[140] (10)

---

[138] Latin: "*Give ear, O my people, to my law*". (*Psalm 77:1*)
[139] *The Office of the Dead*' is said as a prayer for the dead, and is also recited on All Souls' Day, usually November 2nd.
[140] Latin: "*Come let us praise the Lord*". (Psalm 94)

He will say *Matins* and *Lauds* and in place of the verse of the ninth lesson, he will say,

"Libera me, Domine, de timore inferni; nequeant dæmones perdere animam meam, quando illos ab inferis suscitabo, dum illos velle meum imperabo."

That is to say, *"Deliver us, Oh Lord, from the fear of Hell. Let not the dæmons inspire terror in my soul, when I cause them to rise up out of Hell and may I command them to accomplish my will."*

"Dies illa sit clara, sol luceat et luna, quando illos suscitabo"

That is to say, *"May the day be fine and may the sun and the moon shine when I call upon them."*

"Tremendus illorum aspectus horribilis et difformis, Redde formam angelicam, dum illis velle meum imperabo."

That is to say, *"The sight of them is horrible and frightening. Render unto them their* (11) *angelic form, when I command them to do my will."*

"Libera me, Domine, de illis cum visu terribili, et præsta ut sint illi obedientes, quando illos ab inferis suscitabo, dum illis velle meum impeabo."

"Deliver me, Oh Lord, from the terrible sight of them and make them be obedient, when I shall cause them to leave Hell and command them to accomplish my will."

After *The Office of the Dead*, he will extinguish the candle and when the sun rises, he shall cut the throat of a nine day old male lamb, taking care not to let the blood sully the earth. He shall skin the lamb and shall cast its tongue and heart into the fire. The fire will be newly kindled and the ashes shall be preserved, to be used when needed. Spread the skin of the lamb in the middle of a field and for nine days, asperse it with Holy Water four times a day.

On the tenth day, before the rising of the (12) sun, cover the lambskin with the ashes of the heart and tongue and also with the ashes of the cockerel.

On Thursday, after the setting of the sun, bury the flesh of the lamb in a secret place and where no bird may reach[141] and the Priest will write upon the mound with the thumb of his right hand the characters indicated in Figure 3, third line and for three days, he will asperse the four corners with Holy water, saying:

---

[141] Lit. *"come"*.

"Asperges me, Domine, hissopo et mundabor, lavabis me et super nivem dealbabor."[142]

After the aspersion, he will say the following prayer whist upon his knees with his face turned towards the East.

Prayer

"Jesus Christ, Redeemer of Mankind, who being the lamb without blemish, you, who have been sacrificed for the salvation of the human race, who alone were worthy to open the Book of Life, render virtue unto this lambskin, to receive the signs, which we will form thereupon and which shall be written with your (13) blood. May the figures, signs and words have their own efficacious virtue and grant that this skin be a protection against the wiles of dæmons; that at the sight of these figures may they be terrified and may they only approach them trembling. Through You, J.C., who liveth and reigneth through all the Ages. So mote it be."

Then the litanies of the Holy Name of Jesus will be said and in the place of *Agnus Dei*, you will say,

"May the Sacrificed Lamb be our succour against the dæmons.

Slain Lamb, give power over the Power of Darkness.

Sacrificed Lamb, grant favour and strength to bind the rebellious Spirits. So mote it be."

After the lambskin has been stretched for eighteen days, on the nineteenth day, the fleece shall be removed, which shall then be reduced to a powder and which shall be buried in the same place. Write *"vellus"*[143] above it with your finger then the character from Figure 4, Plate III, then continue with: *"Istud (14) sic in cinerem reductum, si præsidium contra dæmones per nomen Jesu".*[144]

Then the characters of fig.6 from the same plate.

Immediately afterwards, set it to dry for three days in the eastern quarter in the sun and with a new knife, cut the characters of the first line of fig. 3, plate II.

---

[142] Latin: *"Asperse me, Oh Lord, with hyssop and I shall be cleansed. Wash me, and I shall be made whiter than snow."* (Psalm 50:9)

[143] Latin: *"Wool".*

[144] Latin: *"May this, which hath been reduced to ashes preserve against the dæmons through the Name of Jesus".*

Having made this figure, recite Psalm 71, "*Deus judicium tuum, regi da etc*"[145] and then cut the character of the same figure on the second line.

After this figure has been completed, recite Psalm 28, "*Offerte Domino patria gentium,*[146] etc." from Psalm 95, "*Cantate Domino canticum*"[147] whose seventh verse is, "*Offerte Domino filii Dei, etc*".[148] Then cut the third line of the same figure.

He will then recite Psalm 77, "*Attendite popule meus, legem meam, etc*".[149] Then he will place onto it figure no. 7 from Plate IV.

With this figure being done, he will say Psalm 2, "*Quare fremuerunt gentes et [populi]*[150] *meditati sunt inania?*"[151]

Finally, cut figure no. 8 (15) from the same plate, after which, recite Psalm 115, "*Credidi propter quod locutus sum.*"[152]

Then on the last Monday of the month, say a *Mass for the Dead*, the prose and the *Gospel of St John* being omitted from it and at the end of the Mass, the Priest will say the Psalm "*Confitemini Domino quoniam bonus etc.*"[153]

"*In the Honour of the Most Holy and Most August Trinity, the Father, the Son and the Holy Ghost. So Mote It Be!*"

The Seventy Two Holy Names of God: "*Trinitas, Sother, Messias, Emmanuel, Sabahot, Adonay, Athanatos, Jesu, Pentagna, Agragon, Ischiros, Eleyson, Otheos, Tetragrammaton, Ely, Saday, Aquila, Magnus Homo, Visio, Flos, Origo, Salvator, Alpha et Omega, Primus, Novissimus, Principium et Finis, Primogenitus, Sapienta, Virtus, Paracletus, Via, Veritas, Vita, Mediator, Medicus, Salus,(16) Agnus, Ovis, Vitulus, Spes, Aries, Leo, Lux, Imago, Panis, Janua, Petra, Sponsa, Pastor, Propheta, Sacerdos, Sanctus, Immortalis, Jesus-Christus, Pater, Filius, Hominis, Sanctus Pater, Omnipotens, Deus, Agios, Resurrectio, Mischiros, Charitas, Æternus, Creator, Redemptor, Unitas, Summum Bonum Infinitas. Amen.*"[154]

---

[145] Latin: "*Render thy Judgment to the king, O God*" (Psalm 71:2).

[146] Latin: "*Give unto the Lord, O ye kindreds of the people.*" (Psalm 95:7).

[147] Latin: "*Sing ye to the Lord a new song*" (Psalm 95:1).

[148] Latin: "*Bring to the Lord, O ye children of God*" (Psalm 28:1).

[149] Latin: "*Give ear, O my people, to my law*" (Psalm 77:1).

[150] This word is missing from the text.

[151] Latin: "*Why have the Gentiles raged, and the people devised vain things?*" (Psalm 2:1).

[152] Latin: "*I have believed, therefore have I spoken*" (Psalm 115:1).

[153] Latin: "*Give praise to Lord, for he is good*" (Psalm 117).

[154] There are seventy names (including Amen which is notariqon for Strong and Faithful King), though two are phrases with two names (Alpha and Omega,

The Figures 9 and 10, Plate IV contain the three small Pentacles of Solomon and the one for the *Gospel of St. John.*

"*Initium Sancti Evangelii Secundum Joannem. Gloria tibi, Domine.*"[155]

Principium and Finis), giving seventy-two in total. The meanings of the names follow, they are all in Latin except where noted: Trinitas (the Trinity), Sother (Saviour), Messias (Messiah), Emmanuel (God be with us (Hebrew)), Sabahot = Sabaoth (Host (Hebrew)), Adonay (Lord (Hebrew)), Athanatos (Immortal (Greek), Jesu (Jesus), Pentagna (unknown meaning, though Penta=five), Agragon (unknown meaning), Ischiros (The Strong One (Greek)), Eleyson (Mercy (Greek)), Otheos = O Theos (O God (Greek)), Tetragrammaton (The Four-lettered Word (Greek)), Ely = El (God (Hebrew)), Saday = Shaddai (Almighty (Hebrew)), Aquila (Eagle), Magnus Homo (Great Man), Visio (Vision), Flos (Blossom), Origo (Source), Salvator (Saviour), Alpha et Omega (First and Last, letters of the Greek alphabet), Primus (First), Novissimus (Utmost), Principium et Finis (Beginning and End), Primogenitus (Firstborn), Sapienta (Wisdom), Virtus (Courage), Paracletus (Comforter (Greek)), Via (the Way), Veritas (the Truth), Vita (the Life), Mediator (Intermediary), Medicus (Healer), Salus (Salvation),(16) Agnus (Lamb), Ovis (Sheep), Vitulus (Bull Calf), Spes (Hope), Aries (Ram), Leo (Lion), Lux (Light), Imago (Image), Panis (Bread), Janua (Door), Petra (Rock), Sponsa (Bride), Pastor (Shepherd), Propheta (Prophet), Sacerdos (Priest), Sanctus (Holy), Immortalis (Immortal), Jesus-Christus (Jesus Christ), Pater (Father), Filius (Son), Hominis (of Man), Sanctus Pater (Holy Father), Omnipotens (Omnipotent), Deus (God), Agios = Hagios (Holy (Greek)), Resurrectio (the resurrection), Mischiros (possibly corruption of Ischiros), Charitas (Charity), Æternus (Without End), Creator (Creator), Redemptor (Redeemer), Unitas (Unity), Summum Bonum Infinitas (the Highest Infinite Good). Amen.

[155] Latin: "*The beginning of the Holy Gospel According to John. Glory be to Thee, Oh Lord!*"

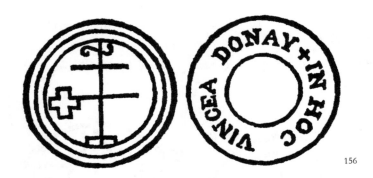

156

"In principio erat Verbum, et Verbum erat apud Deum, et Deus erat Verbum. Hoc erat in principio apud Deum. Omnia per ipsum facta sunt: et sine ipso factum est nihil, quod factum est. In ipso vita erat, et vita erat lux hominum: et lux in tenebris lucet, et tenebrae eam non comprehenderunt. Fuit homo missus a Deo, cui nomen erat Joanes. Hic venit in testimonium et testimonium (17) *perhiberet de lumine, ut omnes crederent per illum. Non erat ille lux, sed ut testimonium perhiberet de lumine. Erat lux vera, quae illuminat omnem hominem venientem in hunc mundum. In mundo erat, et mundus per ipsum factus est, et mundus eum non cognovit. In propria venit, et sui eum non receperunt. Quod quot autem receperunt eum, dedit eis potestatem Filios Dei fieri, his qui credunt in nomine eius: qui non ex sanguinibus, neque ex voluntate carnis, neque ex voluntate viri, sed ex Deo nati sunt. Et verbum caro factum est, et habitavit in nobis: et vidimus gloriam ejus, gloriam quasi unigeniti a Patre plenum gratiae et veritatis.Deo gratias"*[157]

"Hozanna Filio David. Benedictus qui venit in nomine Domini, Hozanna in excelsis. Te invocamus, te adoramus. Te laudamus, te glorificamus.O Beata et gloriosa Trinitas. Sit Nomen Domini benedictum; (18) *ex hoc nunc et usque in seculum, Amen.*

In Nomine Patris, et Filii, et Spiritus Sancti, Jesus Nazarethus Rex Judæorum.

---

[156] Note the missing A before (A)donay

[157] Latin: *"In the beginning was the word, and the word was with God, and God was the word. This was in the beginning with God. All things were made by him: and without him was made nothing, which was made. In him was life, and the life was the light of men: and the light shineth in darkness, and the darkness did not comprehend it. There was a man sent from God, whose name was John. This man came for testimony, to give testimony of the light, that all might believe through him. He was not the light: but to give testimony of the light. It was the true light, which lighteneth every man that cometh into this world. He was in the world, and the world was made by him, and the world knew him not. He came into his own, and his own received him not. But as many as received him, he gave them power to be made the sons of God, to those that believe in his name. Who, not of blood nor of the will of flesh, nor of the will of man, but of God are born. And the word was made flesh, and dwelt in us (and we saw the glory of him, glory as it were of the only begotten of the Father) full of grace and verity. Thanks be to God."*

Christus vincit + regnat + imperat + et ab omni malo me defendat. Amen.[158]

Conjuration Universelle

"Ego N. conjuro te N. per Deum vivum, per Deum verum, per Deum sanctum et regnantem, qui ex nihilo cœlum et terram et mare, et omnia que in eis sunt, creavit in virtute sanctissimi sacramenti Eucharistiæ et nomine Jesu Christi et potentia ejusdem Filii Dei omnipotentis, qui pro redemptione nostra crucifixus, mortuus et sepultus fuit, et tertia die resurrexit, nuncque sedens ad dexteram psalmatoris totius orbis, indè venturus est judicare vivos et mortuos: et te maledicte incirco per judicem tuum tentare ausus Deus est, te exorciso serpens, tibi qui impero, ut nunc et sine mora appareas mihi juxta circulum pulchra et honesta animæ et corporis (19) formâ, et adimpleas mandata mea sine fallacia aliqua.

Nec restrictione mentali per nomina maxima Dei deorum Domini dominantium Adonay, Tetragrammaton, Jehova, Tetragrammaton, Adonay, Jehova, Otheos, Athanatos, Ischyros, Agla, Pentagrammaton, Saday, Saday, Saday, Jehova, Otheos, Athanatos, à Liciat, Tetragrammaton, Adonay, Ischyros, Athanatos, Sady, Sady, Sady, Cados, Cados, Cados, Eloy, Agla, Agla, Agla, Adonay, Adonay.

Constringo te pessime et maledicte serpens N. ut sine mora et legione et gravamine in hoc loco libita signa ante circulum meum sine murmure appareas, sine difformitate nec murmur tione iterum.

Exorciso te per nomina Dei ineffabilia Gogmagogque à me pronuntiari non debuerunt et ternoce mea à lapsu venias adsis N. venias adsis N. venias adsis N."[159] (20)

---

[158] Latin: *"Hosanna to the Son of David. Blessèd is he, who cometh in the name of the Lord, Hosanna in the Highest. We invoke thee, we adore thee. We praise thee, we glorify thee. Oh Blessèd and Glorious Trinity. May the Name of the Lord be blessed; now and henceforth for ever and ever, Amen. In the Name of the Father and of the Son and of the Holy Ghost, Jesus of Nazareth, King of the Jews. May Christ conquer + reign + command + and defend me from all evil. Amen"*
[159] This is a different version of the Universal Conjuration. Latin: *"I, N. do conjure thee Spirit N. by the Living God, by the true God, by the holy and ruling God, who created from nothing the heavens and the earth and the sea, and all that are in them, by the holiest virtue of the sacrament of the Eucharist and the name of Jesus Christ and the power of the same omnipotent Son of God, who was crucified for our redemption, died and was buried, and on the third day rose again, now and sits at the right hand interceding for the whole world, thence he comes to judge the living and the dead: and to judge your evil to prove that he is God, I exorcise you serpents, you who I rule, than now and without delay you appear to me near this circle in true and fair human guise (19), and fulfil my orders without any means of deceit; and not restrict my plans by the great name of the God of Gods Lord of Lords Adonay, Tetragrammaton, Jehova, Tetragrammaton, Adonay, Jehova, Otheos, Athanatos, Ischyros, Agla, Pentagrammaton, Saday, Saday, Saday, Jehova,*

Conjuration

"I, N, do conjure thee Spirit, N. in the name of the Great Living God, who made the Heaven and the Earth and all that is contained herein and by the virtue of the Holy Name of J.-C. His dearest son, who suffered death and passion for us upon the Tree of the Cross, and by the precious love of the Holy Ghost, Perfect Trinity, to appear before me in a human and fair form, without making noise, nor causing any fear. I conjure thee in the name of the Living God Adonay, Tetragrammaton, Jehova, Tetragrammaton, Adonay, Jehova, Otheos, Athanatos, Adonay, Jehova, Otheos, Athanatos, Ischyros, Agla, Pentagrammaton, Jehova, Ischyros, Athanatos, Adonay, Jehova, Otheos, Athanatos, Tetragrammaton, to Luciat, Adonay, Ischyros, Athanatos, Ischyros, Athanatos, Sady, Sady, Sady, Adonay, Sady, Tetragrammaton, Sady, Jehova, Adonay, Eloy, Eloy, Agla, Eloy, Agla, (21) Eloy, Agla, Agla, Agla, Adonay, Adonay, Adonay."

"Veni N.   Veni N. Veni N."

Otheos, Athanatos, to Liciat, Tetragrammaton, Adonay, Ischyros, Athanatos, Sady, Sady, Sady, Cados, Cados, Cados, Eloy, Agla, Agla, Agla, Adonay, Adonay.
I constrain you wicked and evil serpent N. That you appear without noise nor delay and suffering in this place by this agreed sign before my circle, without deformity nor noise again
I conjure you by the ineffable name of God that Gogmagog proclaimed to me and you not keep back and attend to me by hurrying come be present N. Come be present N. Come be present N."
(20)

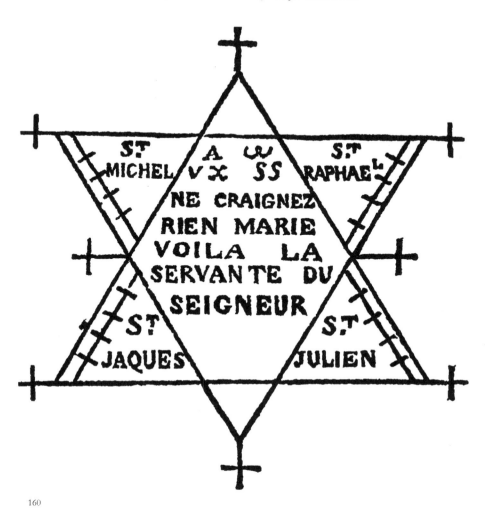

160

---

[160] The hexagon in the centre contains the Greek letters Alpha and Omega and the sequence VXSS, followed by the French words *"ne craignez rien Marie voila la servante du seigneur"*, meaning *"Fear nothing, Mary, behold God's handmaiden"*. The outer triangles contain the names of St Raphael, St Julien, St Jacques and St Michael.

161

---

¹⁶¹ The upper partial circle contains the Latin words *"Spiritus Locus"* – *"Spirit Place"*, and the circles contain the Latin *"Iesus autem transiens per medium illorum ibat ✝ et verbum caro factum est"* meaning *"But Jesus, passing through the midst of them, went His way and the word was made flesh"*, these quotes coming from *Luke 4:30, John 1:14.*

"I conjure thee anew to appear before me by the aforementioned virtues of the powerful and sacred Names of God that I have presently recited in order to achieve my desires and wishes with no falsehood nor lies. Or else, may the Holy Invisible Archangel Michael smite thee into the deepest of Hells. Therefore, N., come to do my will."[162]

AP

"Quid tardatis quid moramini, quid facitis? Preparate vos, obedite præceptori vestro in nomine Domini Bathat vel Rachat super Abrac ruens super veniens Abehor super Aberer."[163]

L.Q.L.F.A.P.

"Behold the Pentacle of Solomon, which I have brought into thy presence and I command thee, by the Great God Adonay, Tetragrammaton and Jesus to fulfil my demands of thee, without wile nor (22) falsehood, but in all truth, in the Name of the Saviour and Redeemer J.-C."

(See the figure for this Pentacle on page 16 of the Works of Agrippa, 1744 edition).[164]

Discharge

"Ite in pace ad loca vestra et pax sit inter vos et vos parati sitis venire vocati. In nomine Patris, et Filii at Spiritus Sancti. Amen."[165]

---

[162] This is part of the Universal Conjuration, but I include it again here as this is an extended version of the Conjuration.

[163] Latin: *"Why dost thou tarry, why dost thou delay, what dost thou do? Prepare yourselves. Be obedient unto your master in the Name of the Lord, Bathat or Rachat coming over Abrac, Abehor over Aberer."* That it is Latin suggests it is taken directly from the *Heptameron*, rather than its derivative in the English of the *Goetia*.

[164] The Pentacle of Solomon is also found in this work in several illustrations.

[165] This is the Latin version of the Discharge that can be found on page 198 [12 of this translation] although the word order is slightly different. *"Go in peace to your place and peace be among you and be ready to come when you are called. In the name of the Father, the Son and the Holy Spirit. Amen."*

Act D.G.[166]

"Laus, honor, gloria et benedictio sit sedenti super thronum et viventi in secula seculorum. Amen."[167]

Conjuration of the Book[168]

"I conjure thee, Oh Book, to be useful and profitable to all those who shall read thee for the success of their affairs. I conjure thee anew, by the virtue of the blood of J.-C. Contained in the Chalice every day, to be useful to all those who shall read thee. I exorcise thee in the name of the Most Holy Trinity, in the name of the Most Holy Trinity, in the name of the Most Holy Trinity."

It is necessary to say that, which follows before the Sealing of the Book[169]

Conjuration of the Dæmons

Editors' note: The rest of these Conjurations in the 1760/1810 edition can also be found in this current translation although the ordering is different. However, there are some variations in the text, which have been highlighted in the appropriate place.

---

[166] Abbreviation for *"Acte de Grâce"* - *"Act of Thanksgiving"*
[167] Latin: *"Praise, honour, glory and blessing be unto him, who sitteth upon the throne and who liveth for ever and ever. Amen."* This may well be derived from *Revelations 4:9*.
[168] Being found on page 184[1]
[169] This is the Conjuration found on page 185 [3], immediately after the Universal Conjuration, which begins *"I conjure and command you Oh Spirits, all and so many as ye are that ye receive this BOOK graciously etc"*.

FROM THE 1670 ROME EDITION.[170]

FOREWORD

Having summoned the magicians from all parts of the world, Honorius The Great asked them to come to Rome, in assuredness of their person, which could only be done with great difficulty, both on account of the insecurity of the roads and also on account of the malice of the Spirits. These then, in truth, drew horrible rains and snows to the country before the magicians arrived in Rome and met each other, all together in this place.

One of them was called Hierosme[171] Adam, coming from the Duchy of Milan, where he was residing in a thick forest. After the conjuration of the Book of Conjurations, whilst in Rome, he performed this operation of speaking to the spirits.

CONJURATION OF THE BOOK

It must be done immediately after the Consecration of the Bread and Wine.

The following words are pronounced:

"I conjure thee, Oh Book, that thou be profitable to those who shall use thee in all their affairs ✚ I conjure thee, by the virtue of the blood of Jesus Christ, who is contained in the Chalice, that thou be good to those who shall read thee."

You should conjure and exorcise the present Book in the way mentioned above, three times in honour of the Most Holy Trinity, then you should complete the Mass.

---

[170] Eliphas Levi's edition has the phrase *"With Eliphas Levi's notes"* written inside the cover. Likewise the words *"corrected by Eliphas Levi - 1856"* were written on the title page. Where such notes occur in the text following, the abbreviation EL will be used to distinguish them.

[171] Alternative spelling for *"Jerôme"*.

WHAT SHOULD BE SAID WHILE MAKING THE PROTECTIVE CIRCLE

During all evocations of Spirits, you should enclose yourself within a circle.

The following formula is pronounced:

"I make the circle to curb and restrain the malign spirit, in the name of the Father ✝, and of the Son ✝, and of the Holy Ghost ✝, that it may be impossible for him to penetrate into the circle, that he may not be able, in any case, to do harm to anyone."

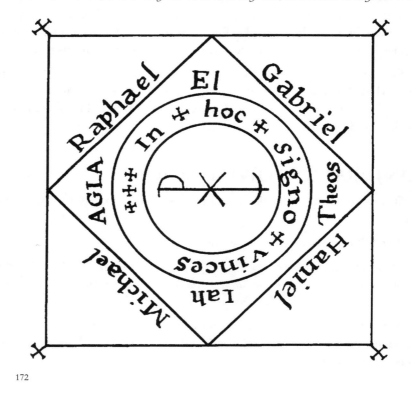

172

---

172 The circle contains the ChiRo representing Christ, surrounded by the words *"In hoc signio vinces"* (Latin) meaning *"In this sign you will conquer"* (referring to the vision of the Roman Emperor Constantine on 28 October 312 CE which subsequently led to his conversion to Christianity. The Hebrew divine names El, Agla and Iah and the Greek Theos surround it, and the outer names are of the archangels Raphael (Air), Gabriel (water), Haniel (Earth) and Michael (Fire).

This circle and the following are traced on the ground. They must be done with charcoal made from consecrated Willow or even, lacking that, with chalk.

The Names of the Hours and of the Angels that preside over them will be found in the High Magic Ritual of H.C. Agrippa.

GENERAL CONJURATION OF THE SPIRITS[173]

"In the name of the Father ✝, and of the Son ✝, and of the Holy Ghost +. Rise up, ye Spirits by the virtue and power of your King, by the seven crowns of your Kings[174] and by the chains under which, all the Spirits of Hell are halted. Constrain N... (indicate the name of such a Spirit that you wish to subjugate) to come to me, without the Circle, to reply to my demands, to do and accomplish all that I shall ask of him according to the power that hath been given to me. Come, therefore, ye Spirits, from the East, as from the West, and make me bring N... Spirits, I thereby conjure you and command you by the virtue and power of He, who is Three Persons Co-Eternal and Co-Equal, who is an invisible and consubstantial God, who created the Heavens and the Earth and all things that are in them through his sole Word."

After this general conjuration, the four following conjurations must be done, which are specific: the first to the King of the East, the second to the King of the West, the third to the King of the South and the fourth to the King of the North.[175]

FIRST SPECIFIC CONJURATION

"Oh Maimon, most mighty King of the East, I call thee and invoke thee to this holy work that I am performing. I conjure thee by the power of all the Names of the Divinity and by the virtue of the Most High, I command thee to swiftly send me and without any delay N... to reply to all that I shall ask of him or even come thou, thyself to satisfy my desire. If thou dost not do so swiftly, I shall thereby constrain thee by the virtue and the power of God, I shall oblige thee to come to respond to all that I wish of thee."

---

[173] Cf. Conjuration of Daemons on p.186 of the main text.
[174] A reference to the seven principle Princes of Hell.
[175] Cf. the conjurations on pages 189 – 191 in the main text.

SECOND SPECIFIC CONJURATION

"Oh King Amaymon, most victorious, who ruleth in the Southern Parts, I call thee and invoke thee by all the Holy Names of God. Come with all thy power, make haste and send me N... before the Circle, otherwise I shall thereby constrain thee by the virtue and the power of the Divine Majesty, by the virtue of the Most Holy and Most Supreme. Satisfy my will promptly without bringing me any distress, or come thyself to respond favourably to all that I ask."

THIRD SPECIFIC CONJURATION

"Oh King Paymon, most potent, who reigneth in the Western Parts, I call thee by all the Names of the Divinity and conjure thee to send me N... swiftly before the Circle. May he inform me and reply to that, which I shall ask of him. If thou dost not do so, I shall torment thee with the Sword of Divine Fire and shall add to thy sufferings."

FOURTH SPECIFIC CONJURATION

"Oh thou Egin, King and Emperor of the Northern Parts, I call thee and invoke thee, I exorcise and conjure thee by the power of the Creator and by the virtue of all the virtues. I desire thee to tarry not in sending me N... in a beautiful and human form."

Having spoken it twice, wherever you may be, you will say:

"Come render honour that thou owest to the Veritable Living God and thy Creator, in the name of the Father + and of the Son + and of the Holy Ghost +. Come, therefore, and be obedient before the Circle, without any peril to myself, neither in body nor soul. Come in a human and beautiful form and not in any way terrible, by all the divine names I adjure thee to call him to come hither forthwith. Thesiel Barachiel, if thou dost not come swiftly, Bolcades suspensus vis ava achare pergalium gaspar, conaootum enim siribam toitee[176] *N... I exorcise thee +. As I invoke thee, I command thee by the power of a living God +, of a True God + and by the force of a Holy God +, as also by the virtue of He, who spake and all things were created: the Heavens, the Earth, the Sea, the Abyss and all that is in them. I adjure thee by the Father + by the Son + by the Holy Ghost + and by the Holy Trinity and by the God against whom thou canst not resist, upon whose empire I shall make thee bow. I conjure thee by God the Father + by God the*

---

[176] This may be an example of nonsense Latin (or Latin glossolalia), that just has to be taken as is, as it is not really translatable at all. Alternatively it may have been transcribed so badly that it has corrupted beyond recognition.

Son **✝**, by God the Holy Ghost **✝**, by the mother of Jesus Christ and perpetual Virgin, by her holiness, by her purity, by her virginity, by her fecundity, by the childbirth, by her virginal belly and by her holy breasts, by her holy womb, by the most holy milk on which the son of the Eternal Father was nourished, by her holy soul and by all the precious members of this virgin and by all her sufferings, passion, afflictions, labours and bitterness that she suffered, while her most cherished son wept, during the time of his painful passion upon the tree of the Cross and by all the holy things that are offered, in Heaven as on Earth, to the honour of Our Lord Jesus Christ and of the blessèd Virgin Mary, his mother, and by all that is celebrated in the Church in honour of God, finally by all the Holy Masses and by all the Mysteries and Signs of the Cross."

WHAT THE MASTER IN THE PROTECTIVE CIRCLE NEEDS YET TO DO

With these Conjurations completed, if the requested Spirit appears, you will make him sign[177] the present Book with the promise to return every time that you call him, then, having given him a gift, you will send him back, saying:

"Retire in peace, without causing harm to whomsoever he may be and be ever ready, at every day and at every hour when I call thee."

Then you need to recite the *Gospel of St John*, *"In principio..."*

If the Spirits are rebellious and nothing appears, you should perform and say the following exorcism:

EXORCISM OF THE SPIRITS[178]

"We, made in the image and likeness of God, endowed with the power of God and made through His will, we exorcise you N... by the almighty, greatly strengthened, potent and admirable name of God El and we command you by He who spake and it was made and by all the names of God Adonay, El, Elohim, Elohe, Zebaoth, Elion, Escherie, Iah, Tetragrammaton, Saday. Lord God Most High, we command you with all power to instantly appear to us around this Circle, in a beautiful form, that is to say, human and with no deformity, nor fault. Thus, come all ye, for we command it of you, by the name of Y and V which Adam heard and which he spake and by the name of God Agla, which Jacob did hear from the Angel with whom he was wrestling and by whom he was delivered

---

[177] In other versions, this refers to the *'Sealing of the Book'*.
[178] This is a version of the Exorcism of the Spirits of the Air from the *Heptameron*.

from the hand of his brother Esau; and by the name Anephexeton, which Aaron did hear and which made him speak and made him wise; and by the name Zebaoth, which Moses named, in the wake of which, all the rivers and swamps were turned into blood; or by the name Eserchie Oreston, which Moses named and who forced all the rivers to eject the frogs that had climbed into the houses of the Egyptians, destroying everything; and by the name Elion which Moses named and which made such heavy hail fall that there has never been anything like it since the beginning of the World; and by the name of Adonay, which Moses pronounced and which brought forth such a prodigious quantity of locusts, which appeared in Egypt and which ate that, which the hail had not destroyed; and by the name Iehemes, Amathia, which Joshua called, which stopped the sun; and by the name Alpha and Omega, which Daniel named, by which he destroyed Bel and slew the Dragon[179]; and by the name Emmanuel which the three children Sidrach, Misach and Abdenago sang in the blazing furnace and by which they were delivered;[180] and by Agios and the seat[181] of Adonay and by, Otheos Ischiros Athanatos Paracletus and by these three secret names: Agla, On, Tetragrammaton, I conjure you and hold you witness, and by all the names, and by all the other names of our Lord Almighty, True and Living God, you who by your sin have been driven from the [high] places, cast into Hell, we exorcise you and command you most strongly by He who, having spoke, all was made, whom all creatures obey. And by the terrible judgements of God, who is to be feared. And by thy sea, which is an element upon which nobody can count on with certainty, transparent like glass, which is in the presence of his Divine Majesty, is ready to rise up following the power that God shall give it thereof. And the four animals of the Throne,[182] who are on the rungs of the Seat[183] of the Divine Majesty, which have eyes in front and behind. And by the fire which surroundeth his Throne. And by the Holy Angels of the places of the Throne. And by that, which is called the Church of God Almighty.

We summon you, with all the power of our will, to appear before this Circle and to obey all that shall please us, by the Seat of Balbachia and by the name Primeumaton, which Moses pronounced and which precipitated in the depths of the Pits of Datan, Coré and Abiron. And by virtue of this name Primeumaton forced by the whole of the Celestial Militia.[184] We curse you, we deprive you of all offices and functions and of all the pleasures that you may have.

We relegate you to the eternal fire and to the lake of fire and sufferings, down to the

---

[179] From *Bel and The Dragon*, one of the Books in the *Apocrypha*.
[180] See the *Canticle of the Three Children in the Furnace* on page 197. Also known as *The Prayer of Azariah* from the Deuterocanonical (Apocryphal) Books of the *Bible*.
[181] Or Throne.
[182] A reference to the four animals in *Revelation* 4:2-11? T may stand for Throne.
[183] Or *"steps of the Throne"*.
[184] St Michael is said to be the Prince of the *"Celestial Militia"*, or Hosts of Heaven.

deepest of the pits and until the last day of the Judgement, if you do not appear, on the spot before the circle to do our will in all things.

Come by these names: Adonay, Zebaoth, Adonay, Amioram. Come, Adonay. Saday commandeth it of you, He, the King of Kings, the most Mighty, the one to be feared the most, from whom, no creature can shield itself from His forces and powers.

If you persist in your extreme obstinacy and if, before the Circle, you do not appear on the spot, affable and courteous, a lamentable and miserable ruin can only await you, as also a fire that can never be extinguished.

Come, therefore, in the name of Adonay Zebaoth, Adonay Amioram; Come, come by Adonay, Saday, the King of Kings. And Aty, Tilep, Azia, Hyn, Jen, Minosel, Achadan, Vay, Vaa, Eye, Haa, Eye, Exe a, El, El, El, a Hy, Hau, Hau, Hau, Va, Va, Va, Va."

WHEN THE SPIRITS APPEAR

You must possess the Pentacle of Solomon, ready to be shown to the Spirits as soon as they appear.

The following words are pronounced:

"Resist not our desires. Be welcome, noble kings and generous princes, all the more so because I have constrained you by the virtue and the power of the One, to whose name all knees bend and bow, who possesseth all the kingdoms, who can suffer no creature to resist his so virtuous power.

I constrain you to remain firm and stable, not to leave from here until you have accomplished my will, point by point.

I constrain you anew, by the virtue of the One, who hath placed boundaries upon the sea, which it hath never exceeded and who, subject to this law, hath never dared oppose the Divine Will. It is the power of this Most High God, King and Lord, who created all things. Amen, in the Name of the Father +, and of the Son +, and of the Holy Ghost +.

Return, now, to your dwelling places may there be peace between us. Such is my sentence."

The Pentacle of Solomon is presented, while pronouncing these words:

"Be ready to come and to disappear each time that I call you."

THE PENTACLE OF SOLOMON

This pentacle is made on virgin parchment. It is consecrated with the

Host. It is the sentence and the condemnation of Spirits. You need to make use of it when they are rebellious and do not wish to reveal the truth without giving any message. It is also good for sending them back: it is shown to them while pronouncing these words: *"Behold your sentence."*

Pentacle of Solomon

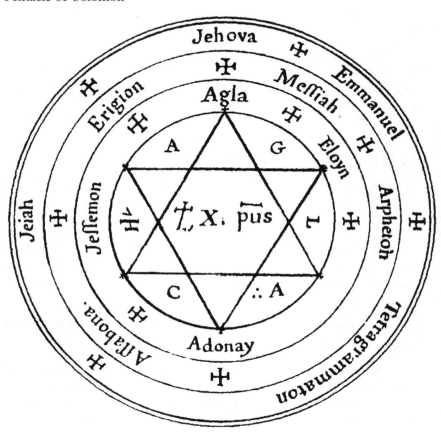

185

---

[185] The Pentacle of Solomon has the divine names Jehova, Emmanuel, Tetragrammaton and Jeiah in the outer ring. The middle ring has the names Messiah, Arpheioth, Assabona and Erigion. The inner ring has the names Agla, Eloyn, Adonay and Jessemon. The letters around the central hexagram (Found in the *Heptameron*) spell the name Agla and CH(r or v), which may be short for Christ or Christos.

CIRCLES AND CONJURATIONS FOR EACH DAY OF THE WEEK TO DIVERSE SPIRITS

FOR MONDAY TO TRINITAS

This operation is performed on a Monday night between 11 o'clock and midnight and between 3 o'clock until 4 o'clock.

You need some charcoal from hallowed willow or some live embers to trace the Circle on the ground, with the words that are around it. You should have a mouse to give him.

The Operator must have a stole and some consecrated water. The conjuration is pronounced with an energetic tone, as the master must do when addressing his servant, prepared to express all manner of threats. Before beginning any invocation, great care will be taken, for your practice, to make the Circle and cense it.

With the preparations having been observed, the following conjuration is pronounced:

"I conjure thee, Lucifer, by the Living God +, by the True God, by the Holy God +, by the God who spake and all things were created.

I conjure thee by the ineffable names of God: Alpha and Omega, El, Eloy, Elion, Ya, Saday, Lux, Omogie Rex Salus Oh Adonay, Emmanuel, Messias."

"I adjure, exorcise and conjure thee by the names declared here-above, by the letters YVEL and by the names Geary, Iol, Iel, Agla, Eizazeris, Oriston, Arphetice Iphaton, Gesmon Yegerson, Isilion, Agiron, Egia, Sperato, Smagon. Anol, Genaton, Sothée, Tetragrammaton, Puermaton, Tionem Pengaron, Yraras, Yaras, Ton Tolaton On Chiros Iron Voy Pheron, Simulaton Penta Rinum Masone.

And by the ineffable names of God Gabin Gauldanum, in godon, Oh blessèd Englabas, mayest thou come or send me N..., in a beautiful human form, without any trouble, nor ugliness, to reveal to me the exact truth concerning all that I shall ask of him, without having the power, of any kind, to harm me in body or soul."

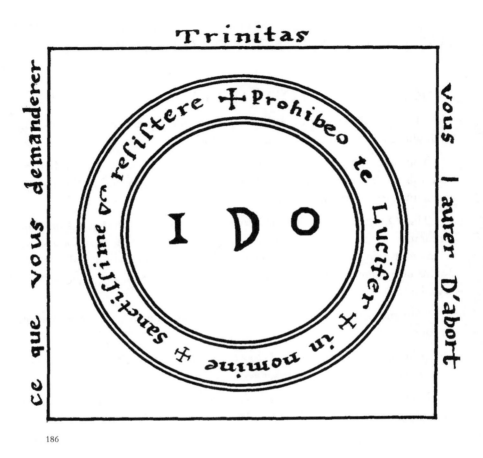

186

FOR TUESDAY TO NAMBROT

This operation is performed at night between nine o'clock and 10 o'clock. In order to be raised up with honour and dignity, the first stone that you find near to yourself will be given to the Spirit as soon as he appears. For the other observations, you will proceed in the same manner as for Monday.

---

186 The inner circle contains a lunar crescent with the letters I and O on either side of it. The Latin words in the circles read *"Prohibeo te Lucifer in nomine sanctissime resistere"* – *"I forbid you Lucifer, in the name of the Most High to resist".* The words in French outside the square read: *"Whatever you will ask for, Trinitas, you will to receive it first."*

Being ready, the following conjuration will be pronounced:

"I conjure thee, Nambrot, and command thee by all the names by which thou mayest be constrained and bound, as also by the power and virtue of the Pentacle of Solomon and by the Chaldean and Celestial Conjurations for confusion and cursing."

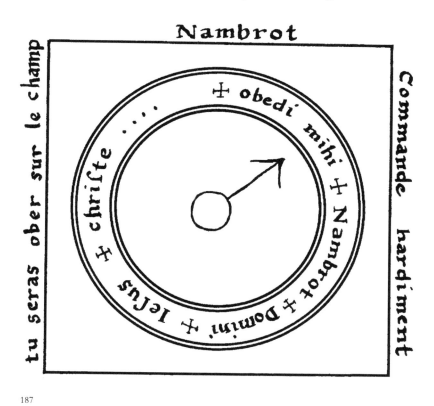

187

"If thou obeyest not my injunction and if thou refusest to accomplish my desires, may thy sufferings and torments redouble and increase, day by day."

---

187 The inner circle contains the symbol for Mars, and the circles contain the Latin words *"Obedi mihi Nambrot Domini Iesus Christe"* meaning *"Obey me Nambrot by our Lord Jesus Christ"*. Outside the square is the French phrase: *"Thou shalt be obeyed in the battlefield, Nambrot, command boldly."*

FOR WEDNESDAY TO ASTAROT

This operation is performed at night, from 10 o'clock until 11 o'clock. In order to obtain the good grace of kings, princes and of powerful men of the Earth, you should give the Spirit a pile of gold. The Spirit appears, then, in the guise of a King.

With the preparations being completed, you will say:

"I conjure thee, malicious Spirit Astarot, by the words and by the Almighty God and by Jesus Christ of Nazareth, under whom all elements are subject, who was conceived by the Virgin Mary, through the ministry of the Archangel Gabriel.

I exorcise thee, anew, in the name of the Father +, and of the Son +, and of the Holy Ghost +, in the name of the glorious Trinity in the honour of whom all the Archangels, Thrones, Dominations, Powers, Patriarchs, prophets, Evangelists, sing without cease."

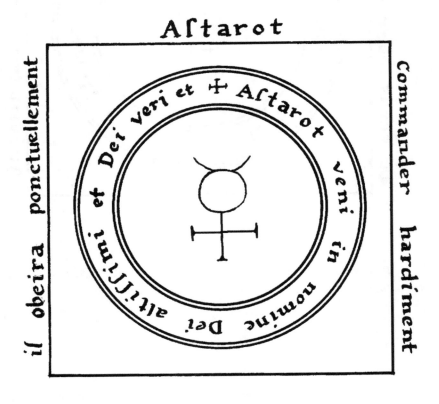

188

---

[188] The inner circle contains the symbol for Mercury, and the circles contain the

"Holy, Holy, Holy Lord God of Hosts, who was, who is and who is to come as a flame of blazing fire, I conjure thee, therefore, Astarot, to obey my commandments and not to refuse to come. I command it of thee by He, who is to come completely in fire, to judge the Quick and the Dead, to whom is due honour, praise and glory. Come, say I, render homage to the True God, to the Living God and to all His creations. Fail thou not to obey me and render honour to the Holy Ghost, for it is in His name that I command thee."

FOR THURSDAY TO ACHAM

This operation is done, equally, at night, between 3 o'clock and 4 o'clock in the morning. The Spirit appears in the form of a King. A little bread should be given to him, if you want him to speak. He makes men happy, especially through possession of treasures.

This conjuration is pronounced:

"I conjure thee, Acham, by the image and likeness of Our Lord Jesus Christ, who, by his dead and passion, redeemed mankind.

By his providence, I wish thee to be here now.

I command thee by the Kingdom of God + Agis + I adjure and constrain thee by His name and by the name of the One, who walked upon the asp and the basilisk, who crushed the lion and the dragon,[189] I adjure and constrain thee to obey me and execute all my commandments."

Latin words *"Astarot veni in nomine Dei altissimi et Dei veri et"* meaning *"Astarot come in the name of the highest God and the true God"*. Outside the square is the French phrase: *"He will obey punctually, Astarot, command boldly."*

[189] These images usually appeared in Late Antique and Early Mediæval art, as Christ trampling on beasts. It is a depiction of *'Christ in Triumph'* having resurrected from the dead and having defeated Satan. It comes from *Psalm 91:13*, *"Super aspidem et basiliscum calcabis conculcabis leonem et draconem"* in the Latin Vulgate: *"The asp and the basilisk you will trample under foot. You will tread on the lion and the dragon".*

Acham

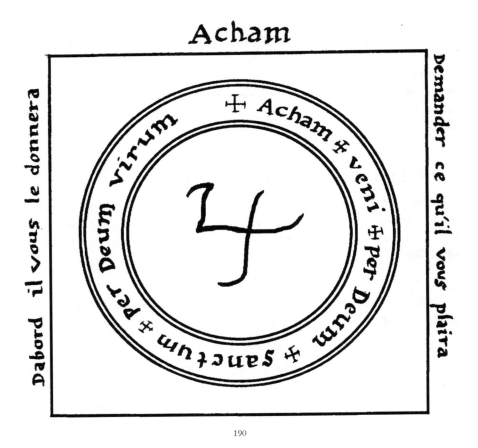

190

FOR FRIDAY TO BÉCHET

This invocation is performed at night between 11 o'clock and midnight. A nut should be handed over.

With the preparations having been carefully observed, the following conjuration will be pronounced:

"I conjure thee Béchet and constrain thee to come to me, I conjure thee anew by the Most Holy Names of God: Eloy + Asinay + Eloy + Agla + Lamasabathani which are written in Hebrew, or Greek, or in Latin, and by all the names expounded in this Book and by the One, who hath driven thee from the Heights of Heaven."

---

190 The inner circle contains the symbol of Jupiter. The circles contain the Latin words *"Acham veni per Deum sanctum per Deum virum"*, meaning *"Acham come by the holy God by the God of men"*. The French outside the square says: *"He will give it to you first, Acham, ask for whatever you please."*

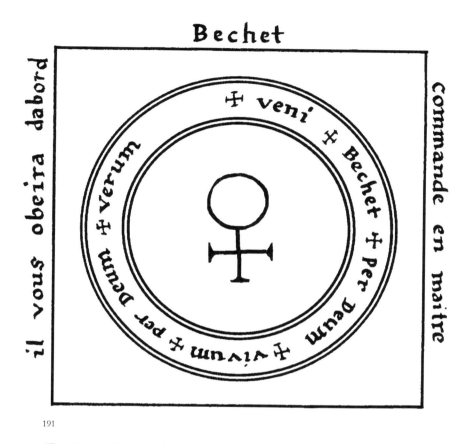

191

"*I conjure and command thee, by the virtue of the Holy Eucharist of Jesus Christ, who hath redeemed men from their sins, that, without delay, to come without any injury to my body, nor soul, without harming my Book, nor anything that I use here against thee and to accomplish all my commandments.*"

FOR SATURDAY TO NEBIROTS

This operation is performed at night from 11 o'clock until midnight. As soon as the Spirit appears, some grilled bread is given to him and ask him what you will.

---

[191] The inner circle contains the symbol for Venus. The Latin words in the circles say "*Veni Bechet per Deum vivum per Deum verum*", meaning "*Come Béchet by the living God by the true God*". The French words outside the square say: "*He will obey you first, Béchet, command as a master.*"

Here is the text of the conjuration in order to constrain him to obey you.

"I conjure thee Nebirots, in the name of Satan and of Belzébuth, in the name of Astarot and of all the other Spirits to come to me. Come now, since I command it of thee in the name of the Most Holy Trinity. I wish thee to come without delay and without injury to either my body, or soul, without harming my books, nor any of the things that I use. Anew do I command thee to appear without delay, or that to send me another Spirit, who may have the same power as thee, who may equally accomplish all my commandments and who may be subject to my desires. May the one, whom thou sendest me, if thou dost not come thyself, not take his leave of me, before having accomplished all that will have been asked of him."

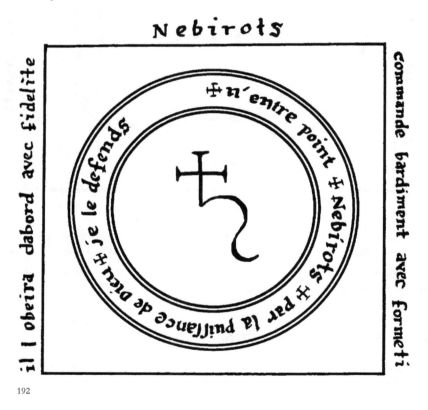

192

---

[192] The inner circle contains the symbol of Saturn. The circles contain the French words "N'*entre point Nebirots par la puissance de Dieu je le defends*", meaning *"Do not enter at all Nebriots, by the power of God I forbid thee"*. The French words outside the square say: *"He will first obey thee faithfully, Nebirots command boldly with firmness."*

FOR SUNDAY TO ACQUIOT

This operation is performed at night, between midnight and one o'clock. When he appears, he will ask for one of your hairs. Give him a hair from a cunning animal, such as the fox, instead. He will be obliged to take it. It is for knowing where treasures are and for anything else that you would want of him.

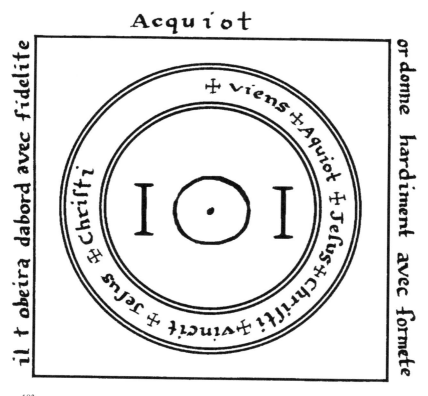

193

---

[193] The inner circle contains the symbol of the Sun between two letter I's. The circles contain the French and Latin words *"Viens + Aquiot + Jesus Christi + vincit + Jesus + Christi"* meaning, *"Come + Aquiot + Jesus Christ + he conquered + Jesus + Christ."* The French words outside the circle say: *"He will first obey thee faithfully, Acquiot, order boldly with firmness."*

The Conjuration to say is:

"I conjure thee Acquiot, by all the names above, to be here swiftly, ready to hear me, or send thou me another Spirit, who will bring me a stone, thanks to which, I may not be seen by anyone when I shall carry it. I conjure thee anew to hold thyself subject to all that I shall command of thee, without injury to my body, nor to my soul.

Come, therefore, and obey me, so that thou mayest know, firstly, the conditions with which I wish to deal with thee, or send me another Spirit, who may execute my desires, point by point, and, above all, who will have found a treasure for me, with which I may be pleased, then, [depart] peacefully."

This conjuration can be performed on any day and at any time, both night and day.

MOST POTENT CONJURATION FOR FINDING HIDDEN TREASURES

This conjuration permits the discoveries of treasures, whether they have been hidden by men or by Spirits. It permits you to find them and to have them brought to you.

Here is the figure of the Circle, which is important to trace on the ground before any operations for evoking. You should stand in the middle.

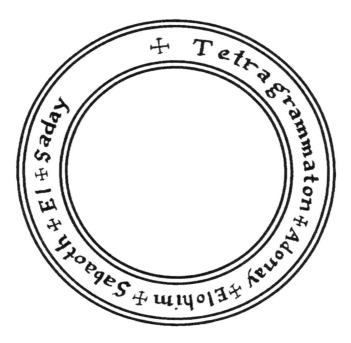

194

With this having been observed, the following conjuration is to be pronounced:

"I conjure you, Dæmons, who dwell in this place, or in whatever part of the world that ye may be and whatever be your power, which hath been given you by God, and the Holy Angels in the Principality of the Abyss, I conjure you all, both generally and also specifically, by the power of God the Father +, by the wisdom of the Son +, by the virtue

---

[194] The circles contain the Hebrew divine names Tetragrammaton Adonay Elohim Sabaoth El Saday.

of the Holy Ghost + and by the authority which is given me by Our Lord Jesus Christ, crucified son of God Almighty, creator of Heaven and Earth, who created us, you and I, from nought, as well as all the other creatures and who by his passion, made it so that you may have no more power to reside in this place, nor to withhold treasures.

I conjure, constrain and command you, that, whether ye like it or not, with no deception, to reveal to me where the treasures may be, which ye have borne away and, by the same authority and by the merit of the Most Holy and Blessèd Virgin Mary and by the One of all the Saints, I expel all you accursed Spirits and send you into the eternal fire, which is prepared for you. If ye are rebellious and disobedient unto me, I command most powerfully for the Devils to torment you."

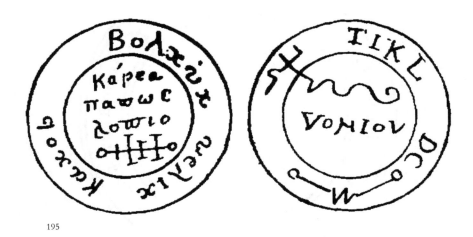

195

"Lastly, by the Holy Names of God Hee + Lahie + Loyon + Hela + Sebaoth + Cheboin + Lodicha + Adonay + Jehova + Ysa + Tetragrammaton + Saday + Messias + Agios + Ischiros + Otheos + Athanatos + Sother + Emmanuel + Agla + Jesus + who is Alpha and Omega +, the Beginning and the End, may they exceptionally torment you and drag you to the deepest and lowest place of the world, where there are insufferable sufferings established precisely in order to punish you for your disobedience to my desires. Lastly, I pray to the Angel Michael to send you to the deepest of the infernal pits.

---

195 As Ioannis Marathakis points out, this is a garbled version of the Taurus seal from Paracelsus' *Archidoxis Magica*, which was subsequently copied into the *Ars Paulina* in the *Lemegeton*.

In the name of the Father +, and of the Son +, and of the Holy Ghost +. Amen."

Here is another conjuration:

"I conjure you, Dæmons all, to withdraw hither unto my words and by all the things that I have spoken above and to forbid you from causing me any fear, fright, terror, nor horror, and not to oppose any creature of God, present or dwelling here.

I conjure you anew, to withdraw without regarding the chains that restrain you in this place and if any Spirits stop you, may the curse of God the Father +, and of the Son +, and of the Holy Ghost +, and may the indignation of the Most Holy Trinity, of all the Angels and of all the Celestial Choir fall and descend upon you, who are rebellious to God.

May not one of these Spirits, therefore, be found here anymore, by the son of God Almighty, Great Jesus Christ, Most High, who reigneth for ever and throughout all the ages. Amen."

DISPOSITION OF THE MASTER

It is important for the Master, who intends to use this Book of Evocations to have a firm assurance of success and to banish from him all incredulity and to perform all the conjurations with such a resolution that whatever may happen to him that is likely to make him afraid, that he has no horror of them.

Above all, he should guard himself when leaving the Circle, and make sure that the Spirits, whether they have appeared to him or not, have been dismissed beforehand, because otherwise, there would be danger.

If he wishes to be a wise magician, let him be on his guard at all times against Spirits' surprises.

Let him not make any illicit pact with them.

Final recommendation: let him command them always boldly, without any fear or apprehension.

FROM THE 1800 ROME EDITION

Note these images are ones which are not found in the other editions, or are different versions thereof.

GRIMOIRE OF POPE HONORIUS WITH A COLLECTION OF SOME OF THE RAREST SECRETS

196

Rome

1800

---

[196] The French words around the edge say *"Obeissez a vos superieurs et leur soyez soumis parce qu'ils y prennent garde"*, which translates as *"Obey your leaders and submit to their authority, for they keep watch over you."* (*Hebrews 13:17*).

136

(26) The Conjuration of the King of the East[197]

---

[197] See the earlier footnote description of the Pentacle of Solomon.

(28) The Conjuration of the King of the North[198]

---

[198] The outer circle contains the French phrase "*Delivrez nous Notre Seigneur Par le Signe de la Croix de nos Ennemis*" meaning "*Deliver us our Lord by the sign of the Cross from our enemies*", and the outside contains two Hebrew divine names separated by the French word *delivrez* - "*Tetragrammaton, Delivrez* [Deliver], *Saday*". The central figure may be a corrupted Saturn sigil.

(46) Very Powerful Conjuration for any day and any hour, Day and Night, for treasures hidden by men as well as by Spirits, to take possession of them or have them transported

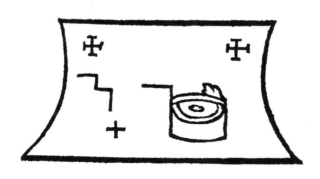

Collection of Secrets

We have used the Collection of Secrets from the 1760 edition as the representative body of text; we have appended some of the more important differences into the text, where appropriate, from the other texts in order to complete it and these additions have been noted in the footnotes. The illustrations are included from the 1670 edition for convenience, as the 1760 edition illustrations to the charms are in the images found in the previous section referred to by plate and figure numbers and may be referred back to. The appendices following it note the main differences.

(48)

COLLECTION OF SOME MOST RARE SECRETS OF THE ART MAGICAL (FROM THE ROME 1760 EDITION)

To see Spirits, of which the air is replete

Take the brain of a cockerel, some powder from the grave of a dead man, that is to say, some dust, which is touching the coffin, some nut oil, some virgin wax and make a concoction from it that you wrap in virgin parchment, into which you will have written these two words: *Gomert Kailoeth* with the following character.[199] Burn it all and you will see some prodigious things. But this should only be done by people, who are fearless.

To win at games

On the eve of St Peter before sunrise, pick the herb called *Morsus Diaboli*.[200] Place it upon a rock that has been consecrated, for a day, then let it dry out. Reduce it into a powder and carry it upon yourself. In order to collect the herb, make a semi-circle with the names and the crosses indicated at fig. 18, plate VIII.

---

[199] There is no *"following character"*, therefore I am assuming that the character is to be found on page 46 of the document

[200] *"Devil's Bit"* or "Smooth *Succisa*", so-called because legend has it that the Devil bit off its short black root. The plant was used to treat Scabies.

201

In order to extinguish a chimney fire[202]

On the chimney, with a piece of charcoal, form the characters and words of the two small pentacles in figure 9, plate IV and pronounce the words[203] over them three times.

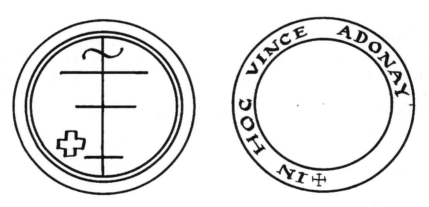

204

---

[201] The charm contains the three Hebrew divine names Adonay, Agla and Jehova.

[202] This charm seems to be derived from *Key of Solomon* manuscripts.

[203] The words are given in the 1670 edition *"In Hoc Vince Adonay"*.

[204] This phrase is missing the word *'signio'* (sign or seal), as it usually reads *"In hoc signio vinces"*, so it would have read *"In hoc signio vinces Adonay"*, or *"Conquer in this name of Adonay"*.

To get gold and silver, or a Hand of Glory[205]

Rip out the hair along with its root from a mare in heat, as close to nature as possible,[206] saying, *"Dragne, Dragne."* Hold onto this hair tightly. Go and immediately buy (49) a newly made earthenware pot along with its cover without haggling for it. Return home, fill this pot with spring water up to two fingers width from the top and place the said hair within. Cover the pot, put it in such a place that neither you nor anyone else will be able to see it, for there might be some danger [if they did]. At the end of nine days and at the same time [of day] that you hid it, go and fetch it. You will find within a little animal in the form of a serpent. It will stand upright. You will immediately say to it, *"I accept the pact."* When you have done that, take it without touching it with your hands, place it in a box, newly and purposely bought without haggling. Place some wheat bran into it, and nothing else, but you should not fail to give him some [wheat bran] every day. And when you wish to have some silver or some gold, place as much [silver or gold] as you wish to have into the box and lie down upon your bed, placing the box next to you. Sleep if you wish (50) for three or four hours. At the end of this time, you will find double [the amount] that you placed in it. But you should be careful to place back the same [amount as before].

Note that the little figure in the form of a serpent only comes through the power of the charm. In this way, you cannot give it more than £100[207] at a time. But if your [Natal] Planet gives you an Ascendant on matters pertaining to Saturn, the serpent will have a face approximating the human form and you will be able to give it up to £1000. Every day, you will draw double from it.[208] If you wish to part with it, you may give it to whomever

---

[205] A Hand of Glory normally came from the severed and dried hand (usually left) of a hanged man whose fingers were used as a candelabra. It was said to possess mystical and magical properties and that the flames of the candles could only be extinguished with milk. It was noted by the etymologist W.W. Skeat (1835 – 1912) that the word derives from the French, *Main de Gloire*, which is a corruption of the French *mandragore*, which is actually a Mandrake, which also has mystical and magical properties associated with it. The invocation *"dragne, dragne"* might be referring to *mandragore*!

[206] That is to say, a wild mare.

[207] Old French Currency, Pounds: £. The Franc, which is better known as a French unit of currency, replaced the Livre (£) in 1360 CE. Charlemagne (or Charles the Great, who established the Carolingian Empire in the 9th century CE) established the Livre (£) in the late 8th Century CE to replace the coinage of the old Roman Empire that was still being used at that time.

[208] The figure from the 1670 Edition on page 22 of the manuscript is found here.

you wish, provided that he accepts, placing the figure that you have with a cross, on the line made on the virgin parchment that is in the box. Or instead of ordinary wheat bran, which is what is generally given to it, it is given bran from wheat, over which a Priest has said his first Mass, then it will die. Above all, do not forget (51) any condition, for there is no mocking in this affair.

Garter in order to travel without tiring oneself [209]

Leave your house whilst fasting, walk on the left-hand side[210] until you have found a merchant of ribbons. Buy an ell[211] of white ribbon. Pay what is asked of you and leave a farthing[212] behind in the shop and return home by the same path. The next day, do the same until you have found a merchant of feathers. Buy a quantity of them, in the same manner that you bought the

---

[209] In the 1670 edition, this *'secret'* is called *"To succeed on a journey"*. This is an expanded version of The Traveller's Garter found in some *Key of Solomon* manuscripts. A version is also found in the later *Black Dragon.*
[210] Presumably, of the road.
[211] A measurement, approximately the length of a man's arm (up to his elbow!). A French ell was 54 inches or 137 cm.
[212] A *farthing* is a coin from that was worth ¼ of a penny or 1/960 of a pound (£) in Old French Currency. See note 192 above.

ribbon. And when you are back in your dwelling, with your own blood, write the characters from fig. 3, plate II on the ribbon for the right garter.[213] Those of the third line are for the left. When this has been done, leave the house. On the third day, wear your ribbon and your feather, walk on the left-hand side until you find a confectioner or a baker. Buy a cake or a two farthing (52) loaf of bread. Go to the first tavern and ask for a quarter of a pint[214] of wine, have the glass rinsed three times by the same person, break the cake or the bread into three pieces and put the three pieces into the glass with the wine. Take the first piece and throw it under the table without looking, saying *"Irly, for thee"*. Then take the second piece and throw it, saying *"Terly, for thee"*. On the other side of the garter, write the name of these two Spirits with your blood. Throw the third piece, saying, *"Firly, for thee"*. Throw the feather away, drink the wine without eating, pay your share of the bill and leave. When you are outside the town, put on your garters. Take care not to make any mistake by placing the garter for the right leg on the left, as there will be consequences. Strike the earth three times with your foot, while calling on the names of the Spirits, *"Irly, Terly, Balthazard, Melchior, Gaspard, let us go"*. Then go on your journey. (53)

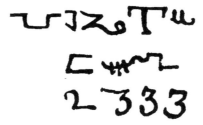

To be impervious against all manner of weapons

Take some water that has been blessed during Easter and some wheat flour. Make a dough from it and look for someone who is about to die a violent death, such as being hanged or by any other legal punishment. Approach as closely as you can to him and without saying anything, hold your dough up in the air. Then when you have judged that he has passed

---

[213] The characters are found on page 23 of the 1670 edition.
[214] Lit. a *"half-setier"*. A *setier* is an ancient measurement. The quantity varies from country to country but it is roughly a quarter of a pint. From the Latin *sextarius* – a *"sixth"*.

away, conjure his spirit to come and be enclosed in your dough in order to protect yourself against all manner of weapons. Return home and make some small dumplings. Wrap them in some virgin parchment, onto which you will have written the following: "*1. u,n., 1., a. Fau, 1. Moot, and Dorhort. Amen.*" You have to swallow these dumplings.

While making the dumplings, you have to say the *Pater* five times and the *Ave* etc. five times.

Note: that the number of these dumplings is arbitrary and that the preceding characters are written on a single piece of virgin paper (54), you should share as many parts of the dumplings that you make as you can. The baptismal name of the patient should be named in the conjuration.

Conjuration to the Sun

Take a piece of paper and make a hole in it and look through it towards the rising sun, saying, "*I conjure thee, Solar Spirit, on behalf of the Great Living God, that you may let me see N.*" Then continue in this manner, "*Anima Mea turbata est valde; sed tu, Domine, usquequo.*"[215] Repeat three times.[216]

---

[215] One of the Seven Penitential Psalms in the Bible. *Psalm 6*: *"My soul is also sore vexed: but thou, O Lord, how long?"*
[216] The following image is from the 1800 edition.

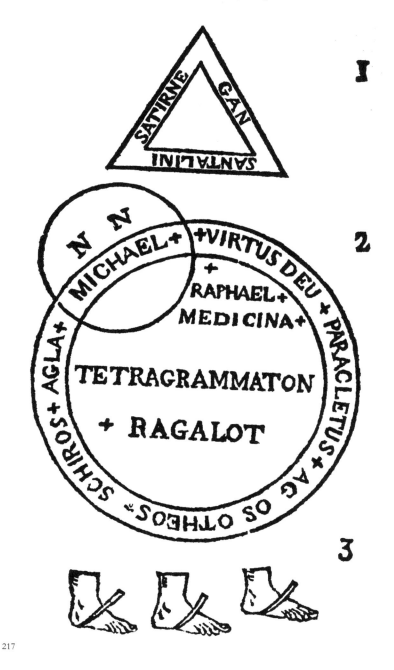

I

2

3

217

---

217 The outer circle contains the phrase Virtus Deu (the Might of God, Latin referring to Michael as the translation of his name), and divine names some of

To see a vision in the night of what you wish to see, in the past or the future

On the two NN. that you see in the inner circle of fig.22, plate X mark the place where you should put your name. And in order to know what you desire, write the names that are in the circle on virgin parchment, doing everything before going to sleep then place it on your right ear, look at the sunset and say the following prayer three times: (55)

Prayer

"In the glorious name of the Great Living God, to whom at all times, all things are present to him, I who am your servant N. Eternal Father, I beg you to send me your angels that are written in the circle and may they show me that, of which I am curious to know and learn, through J.-C.O.-S.[218] So mote it be."

With the prayer finished, retire to bed and sleep on your right side and you will see what you desire in a dream.

To use a nail to make someone suffer

Go to a cemetery and there, collect a nail from an old coffin, saying, *"Nail, I take thee so that you may serve me to divert and cause harm to any person that I wish. In the name of the Father, the Son and of the Holy Ghost. Amen."*

When you wish to make use of it, find the [victim's] footprint and make the characters from fig.20 plate IX,[219] then drive the nail into the middle of the little triangle from (56) the figure, which you will have traced on a strip of plank, saying the *Pater Noster*[220] until *"in terra".*[221] Knock the nail in with a rock, saying, *"May you cause harm to N. until I pull you out from there."* Cover the place with a little powder and take a good note of where it is, as you can

---

which are corrupted; thus Paracletus, Ag Os (Agios), Otheos, Schiros (Ischiros) and Agla, with the name of the archangel Michael in the part which overlaps with the circle for conjuration of the spirit, echoing the use of his name in the triangle to constrain demons in the *Goetia*. The inner circle contains the names Raphael, Medicina (Latin short for Medicina Dei or God's Healing, the translation of Raphael, Tetragrammaton and Ragalot

[218] Jesus Christ our Saviour, The French uses the abbreviation J.-C.N.-S.: *"Jésus Christ Notre Sauveur."*

[219] The characters are found on page 26 of the 1670 edition.

[220] The Lord's Prayer.

[221] Latin: *"on Earth".*

only heal the harm that it causes by pulling the nail out from that place and saying, *"I retract thee so that the harm that thou hast caused N. ceases. In the name of the Father, of the Son and of the Holy Ghost, Amen."* Then pull out the nail and rub out the characters, not with the same hand with which you made them, but with the other, because there might be some danger to the wielder of the evil spell.

To make oneself appear to be accompanied by many

Take a fistful of sand and conjure it thus, *"Anachi, Jehova, Hælersa, Azarbel, rets caras sapor aye pora cacotamo lopidon ardagal margas poston eulia buget Kephar, Solzeth Karne phaca ghedolossalese tata."* Place the sand thus conjured into an ivory box with the powdered skin (57) of a Tiger Serpent. Then throw it into the air while reciting the conjuration and there will appear as many men as there are grains of sand; do this on the day and at the hour when the sun is in the Sign of Mary, the Virgin.

Not to be wounded by any weapon

Recite all of this in the morning. *"I rise in the name of J.C. who hath been crucified for me. May it be Jesus' desire to bless me. May it be Jesus' desire to lead me. May it be Jesus' desire to guard me well. May it be Jesus' desire to govern me well and lead me to Life Eternal, in the name of the Father and of the Son and of the Holy Ghost."* It should be said three times before retiring to bed and before rising. The following should be written on the sword or weapon, which you wish to use: *"Ibel, Ebel, Abel"*.

To make a weapon fail

Take a new earthenware smoking pipe, whose chamber-cover[222] has been trimmed with brass, fill it with powdered Mandrake root,[223] then puff on the pipe while pronouncing silently to yourself, *"Abla, Got, Bata, Bata, blue."* (58)

---

[222] Literally, Cover-Fire - *"couvre-feu"*. This is where the English word *'curfew'* comes from.
[223] Mandrake is known to have narcotic and hallucinogenic effects when inhaled. The root itself was often carried on a person as a protective amulet.

For Pleurisy

In a bottle of fine white wine, let ten to twelve pieces of horse, donkey or mule droppings infuse on top of a bundle of glass wool[224] for two hours. While still hot, after you have poured and squeezed this liquid out, pour it into a glass at the bottom of which you will have written beforehand, "*Dia, Bix, On, Dabulh, Cherih.*" Drink it in a well-covered bed and the next day you will be healed.

For fevers[225]

Dissolve half an ounce of green Couperose[226] in a glass of water. With this solution, write the words on a piece of paper as big as the thumb: "*Agla, Garnaze,*[227] *Eglatus, Egla.*" Swallow similar slips of paper for five days in a row. Take the following preparations for five days:

For intermittent fever

Before bouts of fevers, take a sugared pill of powdered root of the Great Yellow Gentian.[228] (59)

For tertiary fever[229]

Take some hound's-tongue root[230] newly extracted from the earth, cleaned and sliced, and apply it over your navel with a cloth over it to hold it in place. Renew it every twelve hours.

---

[224] Or literally "*sand wool*". Presumably, it is being heated up.

[225] In the 1670 Edition, this is called "*Against all fevers*".

[226] Also known as "*Blue Stone*", this is Copper Sulphate ($CuSO_4$), which is coloured blue.

[227] EL: Garnaze -> Garnaza.

[228] This herb was mainly used as a general tonic for digestive disorders, but it was also thought to be effective for general debilitating chronic illnesses.

[229] Fevers caused by infectious agents: usually syphilis and malaria during this period in history

[230] *Cynoglossum officinale*. It was called dog's tongue or *houndstongue* because of the belief that it could ward off attacks from dogs when it was carried in the shoe. It was used in herbal medicine for diseases of the lungs, including coughs. It was also used for piles when taken internally. As an ointment, it was used to cure baldness and treat ulcerous and other lesions on the skin.

For quartan fever[231]

At the start of the bout, take a sugared pill of Myrrh[232] in a glass of white wine. Repeat three times.

To stop loss of blood

Write "*INRI*" with blood on a piece of paper, which you apply to your forehead. Then avail yourself of some powder, which exudes from the cavity of the dried fruit of the plant called Puffball,[233] mixed with egg white. If the loss [of blood] is occurring internally, such as spiting and vomiting of blood, put some alum powder in a preserve of red roses and eat some of it in the morning whilst fasting and in the evening while going to bed until you have been healed. (60)

Against a sword strike

Before going to fight, write the two words on a ribbon of any colour whatsoever: "*Buoni jacum.*"

Hold on fast to this ribbon in your fist, be fearless, protect yourself and the sword of your enemy will never touch you.

For when you are going into action[234]

Say five *Pater* and five *Ave* in honour of the Five Wounds of O.S.[235] Then say three times, "*I take my leave in the chemise of Our Lady. May I be surrounded by the Wounds of my God, by the four Crowns of Heaven, by the Lord St John the Evangelist, St Luke, St Matthew and St Mark. May they guard me; may no man, woman, lead metal, iron, nor steel wound me, cut me up, nor crush my bones, for the sake of God's Peace.*" And when the above has been recited, you have to swallow the following words [written] on white Corncockle:[236] "*Est principio,*"

---

[231] Malaria.

[232] Myrrh is well known for its antibiotic effects. However, modern scientific research has also demonstrated that Myrrh has anti-schistosomal properties and is effective against the parasites that cause malaria.

[233] A type of mushroom, often found in a *'fairy ring'*, usually edible and its spores were used in folk medicine to stop bleeding.

[234] In the 1670 Edition, this *'secret'* is called *"to be sheltered from all nasty action"*.

[235] Our Saviour.

[236] *Agrostemma githag* A poisonous plant used in folk medicine.

est in principio est in verbum, Deum et tu (61) phantu.'[237] It is good for twenty four hours.

To extinguish fire[238]

Say, *"Great, ardent fire, I conjure thee by the Great, Living God, to lose thy colour as did Judas, when he betrayed Our Lord on the Day of Good Friday. In the Name of the Father and of the Son and of the Holy Ghost."* It is repeated three times, while giving the fire a kick with the foot or a poke with the fist, and as much cut hay as can be procured that has been well soaked [in water] is thrown onto the fire.

For burns[239]

"Fire, lose thy heat, as Judas did lose his colour, when he betrayed Our Saviour in the Garden of Olives." This is pronounced three times over the burn, blowing on it each time. Then wrap the burn with a thick wad of compressed cotton wool, or place a compress of strong wine vinegar[240] on top of it, which you renew every two (62) hours for the first day and every six hours on the following days.

For headaches

Take some powdered black pepper,[241] mix it with some good *eau-de-vie*[242] to make a kind of gruel out of it. Spread it on a headband, which you apply to your forehead while pronouncing the words three times, *"Millant, Vah, Vitalot."* Then say three *Pater*.

---

[237] Latin: *"He is the beginning, he is in the beginning, he is in the Word, God and thou Spirit"*.
[238] In the 1670 Edition, this is called *"To extinguish interior fire"*. This charm is also found in the *Enchiridion of Pope Leo III*.
[239] In the 1670 Edition, this is called *"To heal a burn"*.
[240] Vinegar was often used as an antiseptic.
[241] Black pepper is better known for its medicinal effects on the digestive system. It was also used for colds and sore throats.
[242] That is to say, Brandy.

For Stomach Flux[243]

Whilst fasting, it is necessary to drink four ounces of purified plantain[244] juice for three days in a row and say the following each time:

"I have entered into the Garden of Olives, I have met Saint Elizabeth there, she spoke to me of her stomach flux, I asked for her grace for my own and she commanded me to say Pater three times and Ave three times in honour of God and St. John." (Say three *Pater* and three *Ave*, as (63) it is stated here and you will be healed.)

To prevent [someone] from eating at the table[245]

Nail into the underside of the table, a needle that might have been used to bury a dead man and which may have pierced his flesh. Then say, *"Coridal, Nardac, Degon."* Then you will place a piece of asafœtida onto burning charcoal and you will withdraw.

To extinguish fire[246]

In place of the words indicated on page 61, say these following words, having made the sign of the Cross: *"Anania, Anassia, Emisael, libera nos Domine."*[247] Then cast the cut and wet straw [over it], as has been mentioned.

To prevent copulation

For this operation, you will need a new pocket knife. Then on a Saturday, at the precise hour of Moon Rise, while it is waning, trace the characters of figure 5 (64), Plate III with the point, as well as these words, *"Consummatum est,"*[248] on the back of the door of the room where the persons sleep and then break the point of the pocket knife in the door.

---

[243] In the 1670 Edition, it is just called *"To stop the flux"*.

[244] This would refer to the *Plantago* plant, which shares its name of Plantain with the unrelated species of banana. The herb has been used as an anti-inflammatory and its seeds, when ground up, have been used for digestive disorders. It is usually known by its other more familiar name, *Psyllium*.

[245] The *'someone'* is added in the 1670 Edition but is missing from the other editions.

[246] In the 1670 Edition, the a Sign of the Cross is made between the names *"Anania + Anassia + Emisael + libera nos + Domine"*.

[247] Latin: *"free us, o Lord"*.

[248] Latin: *"It is completed"* or *"it is done"*.

For Games[249]

During stormy weather, gather some clover with four or five leaves, making the sign of the Cross over them. Then say, *"Oh wide-leaved Trefoil, or Clover,*[250] *I gather thee in the Name of the Father, and of the Son, and of the Holy Ghost, by the virginity of the Holy Virgin, by the virginity of St John the Baptist, by the virginity of St John the Evangelist, that thou mayest aid me in all manner of games."* You need to say five *Pater* and five *Ave*, then you continue, *"El, Agios, Ischyros, Athanatos."* Keep this clover in a sachet of black silk, which you carry as you would a scapular[251] for every time that you play. At other times, you should take care to keep it carefully pressed.

To stop a serpent[252]

Throw a piece of paper that has been dipped in a solution of alum[253] at it and on which you will have (65) written with the blood of kid goat, *"Stop, Fair One, behold a forfeit."* Then with a wicker whistle, whistle at it. If it is affected by this whistle, it will then die on the spot, otherwise it will promptly flee.

For ringworm of the hair[254]

For ten days, say that, which follows: *"Saint Peter sat down on the Bridge of God.*[255] *Our Lady of Caly*[256] *came thither and said to him, 'Peter, what dost thou there?' 'Lady, it is on account of the hurt of my master that I am placed here.' 'St.*

---

[249] In the 1670 Edition, this is called *"To win at games".*

[250] Also associated with the *'Shamrock'.* This leaf was considered most auspicious when it was found with 4 leaves instead of the usual three. Four-leaved clovers are still considered to bring luck today.

[251] A Christian Sacramental item: It was a length of cloth that hung down both the front and back of the Priest (or nun), draped across the shoulders.

[252] In the 1670 Edition, this is called *"To stop a serpent in its tracks".*

[253] Alum was often used to treat snake bites; it was usually ingested.

[254] *Tinea capitis.* This charm is also found in *Les Oeuvres Magiques* d'Henri Corneille Agrippa, 1744:100.

[255] *The Bridge of God* is a bridge of stone that has been naturally carved over a river or a gorge.

[256] We cannot find any clear reference to Caly. It is possible that it is the name of a place in France, in which case it may be an alternative spelling for Cally. Interestingly, there is a place in Scotland in Perthshire, called Bridge of Cally.

Peter, thou shalt rise up, to St Ager[257] *shalt thou go. Thou shalt take some sacred ointment from the mortal wounds of Our Lord. Thou shalt smear thyself with it and thrice shalt thou say, "Jesus, Mary" and thrice shalt thou make the Sign of the Cross on thy head."* After these words, apply a hot poultice of stewed watercress[258] with pork fat three times on your head.

For games of dice

"Dice, I conjure you in the name of Assizer and of Rassize, that they may come (66) raid and grab[259] *in the names of Assia and of Longrio."* Note well, that you need to be a bearer of the scapular[260] formed from clover leaves, as is mentioned on page 64.

To remove a fish-bone from the throat

A medium-sized leek is used, whose roots or filaments have been cut away. For this purpose, it is dipped in salad oil and inserted into the gullet, repeatedly if need be, while pronouncing these words, *"Blaise*[261] *martyr and servant of Jesus Christ, I command thee to rise up or hurtle downwards."*

Not to tire of walking

Write on three silk ribbons, *"Gaspard, Melchior, Balthazard."*[262] Tie one of

---

[257] Possibly St Auger, a little known saint, who was an anchorite and colombanist monk (i.e. one that withdraws from society for religious reasons) who later became a bishop. Colombanist possibly refers to a follower of St Columba, who was one of the 12 Apostles of Ireland and lived in the 6th century CE.

[258] The juice of Watercress was often used to treat infections of the skin and was also used for hair loss.

[259] Presumably to grab and swipe all the winnings.

[260] A devotional item used in Christianity, worn front and back over the shoulders and reaching to the knees.

[261] St Blaise was a martyred Armenian saint from the 3rd and 4th centuries CE. He was martyred by first being beaten and then beheaded. During the Middle Ages, he was one of the *'Fourteen Holy Helpers'* or *'Auxiliary Saints'* (Saints thought to be able to intercede effectively for various diseases – St Blaise was a noted physician.). St. Blaise was thought to help diseases of the throat, which is why he is more than likely invoked here and also to protect domestic animals.

[262] Traditionally the names of the three Magi from the *New Testament* that visited the newborn infant Jesus. See *Matthew 2:1–12.* While the names *per se* are not mentioned in the *New Testament*, these are the names that The Western Christian Tradition gives

the ribbons above the right knee without tightening it; the second above the left knee and the third around the small of the back. Before setting off, swallow a small glass of aniseed[263] in some broth or in a glass of white wine, (67) and rub your feet with some crushed rue[264] in olive oil.

To win at all games

We have already made several ways of winning games known on pages 48, 64 and 65. Here is another one of them, which we found in an old manuscript. We have not yet been able to judge its worth.

Write the following words and crosses on virgin parchment, "**+** *Ibel* **+** *Laber* **+** *Chabel* **+** *Habet* **+** *Rabel.*" You need to carry it upon your person.

To break and destroy all evil spells[265]

Take an amount of salt, more or less equal to the quantity of the cursed animals. Pronounce over it that, which follows: "*Herego gomet hunc gueridans sesserant deliberant amei.*"[266]

Circle the animals three times, beginning on the side of the rising sun and continue, following the course of this Star with the animals in front of you and while casting pinches of salt onto them, recite the same words. (68)

The Great Exorcism to dispossess either the human creature or irrational animals

"Dæmon, leave the body of N. by the order of God, whom I adore and yield to the Holy Ghost. I place the sign of the Holy Cross of Our Lord J.-C. On your forehead. In the Name of the Father and of the Son and of the Holy Ghost. I make the Sign of the Cross of O.-L. J.-C. over your chest. In the Name of the Father and of the Son and of

---

to them.

[263] Anise was mainly used as a Carminative, that is to say, against flatulence.

[264] Rue was used as an insect repellent. However, it often caused blisters when applied to the skin.

[265] In the 1670 Edition, this is entitled *"Another, to destroy all curses affecting animals".*

[266] This is a case of *"made up"* Latin as it is nonsensical but appears to have some words from Occitan, such as *"gueridans"*. Pissier (2011:75) comments on the unclear meaning of this phrase. EL: "*Par hoc ego me + hunc Savans + cesserunt a me qui nocere deliverant.*" This contains an uncertain word (savans), so reads: *"Through this I + those that know? + they shall go from me and deliver me from harm."*

the Holy Ghost. Eternal and Almighty God, Father of O.-L. J.-C., cast your eyes of mercy upon your servant N, whom you have deigned to call to the right hand of the faith, heal his heart from all manner of elements and misfortunes and break all his chains and bonds. Open, Oh Lord, the gate of your glory by your bounty, so that, being marked with the seal of your wisdom, he may be free from stench, from attacks and from desires of the unclean spirit, and being filled with the sweet odour of your kindness and grace, may he observe your commandments with joy (69) in your Church. And while advancing from day to day in perfection, may he be rendered worthy to have received the beneficial remedy to his faults, by your holy baptism, by the merits of the same J.-C. O.-S. and of God. Lord, we beseech you to grant our prayers, to preserve and protect the very same with a charitable love, who hath been redeemed with the price of your precious blood and by the virtue of your Holy Cross, by which we are marked. Jesus, Protector of the wretched and afflicted, be favourable unto the people, whom you have adopted, making us participants of the New Testament, so that the letters of the promise may be granted and received by your grace that they can only hope for through you J.-C. O.-S., who are our recourse, who have made the Heavens and the Earth. I exorcise thee, Oh creature, in the Name of God, the Father Almighty and by the love that Our Lord Christ Jesus[267] beareth, and by the virtue of the Holy Ghost; I exorcise thee by the Great Living God, who (70) is the true God, whom I adore, and by the God, who hath created thee, who hath preserved all his chosen ones, who hath commended his servants to bless him, to the benefit of those who believe in him, so that everything may become a salutary Sacrament to drive out the enemy. It is for that reason, Oh Lord our God, that we beseech you to sanctify this salt by your holy benediction, and to render it a perfect remedy for those, who shall receive thereof. May it remain in their bowels, so that they may be incorruptible, in the Name of O.-S. J.-C., who is to judge the Quick and the Dead, and by the seal of the God of Abraham, of the God of Isaac, of the God of Jacob, of the God of whom appeared to his servant Moses upon Mount Sinai, who lead the children of Israel out of Egypt, giving them an Angel to protect them to lead them by day and by night. I pray to you also, Oh Lord, to send your Holy Angel to protect your servant, N. and to lead him to life eternal, by the (71) virtue of your Holy Baptism. I exorcise thee, Oh impure and rebellious Spirit, in the Name of God the Father, of God the Son, of God the Holy Ghost. I command thee to leave the body of N., I adjure thee to withdraw in the Name of the One, who gave his hand to Saint Peter when he was close to sinking into the water. Obey thy God, Oh accursed dæmon, and obey the sentence that hath been pronounced against thee, and render honour unto the Living God, render honour unto the Holy Ghost and unto J.-C., the only-begotten son of the Father. Be gone, Oh ancient serpent, from the body of N. for the Great God commandeth it of thee. May thy pride be confounded and crushed before the

---

[267] This is an acronym: NCJB. It might be Notre Christ Jesus B? Or it could be a copying error and should be NSJC (OSJC).

Ensign of the Holy Cross, by which we have been marked through the baptism and grace of J.-C. Consider this, that the day of thy torture approacheth and that unbearable torments await thee, that thy judgement is irrevocable, that thy sentence condemneth thee to the everlasting flames, as well as all thy companions, on account of your rebellion towards your Creator. (72) It is why, Oh accursed Dæmon, I command thee to flee for the sake of God, whom I adore. Flee, by the Holy God, by the True God, by the One, who spake, and all things were made. Render honour to the Father, to the Son and to the Holy Ghost, and to the Most Holy and Most Undivided Trinity. I command thee, Oh unclean Spirit, whosoever thou mayest be to leave the body of this creature, N. created by God, who is the same God, N.-S.J.-C., that today he may deign by his infinite bounty, to call thee to the grace of participating in his holy Sacraments, which he hath instituted to the salvation of all the faithful. In the Name of God, who will judge the whole World by fire.

Behold the Cross of O.-S. J.-C. + Flee, opposing parties, behold the Lion of the Tribe of Judah, Root of David."[268]

To remove all spells and to summon the person who caused the evil deed

Take the heart of one of the dead animals. There should absolutely be no sign (73) of life. Rip out the heart, place it on a clean plate, then get nine hawthorn barbs and proceed as follows:

Lance the heart with one of your barbs, saying, *"Adibaga, Sabaoth, Adonay, contra ratout prisons pererunt fini unixio paracle gossum."*[269]

Take two of your barbs and use them to lance [the heart], saying, *"Qui sussum mediator agros gaviol valax."*

Take another two of them and while using them to lance [the heart], say, *"Landa zazar valoi sator salu xio paracle gossum."*[270]

---

[268] See *Revelations 5:5*.

[269] All of the phrases in this charm have elements of Latin in them, but they do not make sense as a lot of the words seem to be either corrupted beyond recognition, or made up, with elements of the Langues d'Oc in them. The words Sabaoth and Adonay are the Hebrew for Lord of Hosts (Adonay Sabaoth). EL: *"Contraire à touts poisons* [Fr: *Antidote to all poisons*] – *Semper erunt + finis + uni X to + paracletus + ego sum"*. This Latin reads: *"They shall be forever + the End + the only X [Christ] + the Comforter [Holy Spirit} + I am"*.

[270] This phrase includes the word Sator, which is well known as part of the Sator magic square charm, and Paracle, which is clearly an abbreviation of the Greek word Paraclete, meaning Comforter and used as a title of the Holy Spirit.

Continue with two more of your barbs and while using them to lance [the heart], pronounce, *"Mortus cum fice sunt et per flagellationem Domini nostri Jesu-Christi."*[271]

Finally, use the last two barbs to lance [the heart] with the words that follow: *"Avir sunt devant vous paracletur strator verbonum offisum fidando."*[272]

Then continue, saying,

"I call upon the persons, men or women both, who have made the fabrication of the Missal of Abel. Let it be, it was poorly done that leaving, thou mayest come and find us by sea or (74) by land, all of you everywhere, without delay and without forfeit. Pierce for now the heart of a nail to its last words."[273]

Note, that if you cannot get hawthorn barbs, use nine nails in their stead.

With the heart being pierced, as we have indicated, it is placed into a small sack. Then it is taken to the fireplace. The next day, you will take the heart out of the sack, place it on a plate, removing the first thorn and piercing the heart it anew in another place, pronouncing the words that we have assigned to it above. You will remove two others and piercing it again, say the appropriate words. Then you take them all out in the same order and use them to re-pierce the heart, as we have said, making sure that you never lance the same hole twice. Continue this operation for nine days. Each time you do it, if you still do not wish to release your malefactor, you will perform your *Novena*[274] (75) on the same day and in the order prescribed in the last operation. You will pierce the heart with the nail, pronouncing the words that we have assigned to it for the purpose at hand. Then a great fire is made and the heart is placed on a grill in order to roast it over the glowing embers. The malefactor should come to ask for pardon. Or if it is outside of his power to come in the little time that is granted him, you will cause him to die.

---

[271] Latin, roughly: *"They are marked with death and by the scourging of our lord Jesus Christ."*
[272] Corrupt Latin, roughly: *"Avir(?) are before you the Comforter [by name of the Holy Spirit] ???? by believing."*
[273] The language for this particular passage was garbled and nonsensical. Its actual meaning is unclear. But it may be that this was the author's intention.
[274] This is a Catholic devotional prayer that is repeated on nine consecutive days.

The Castle of the Fair, a guard for horses[275]

Place some salt on a plate. Then with your back turned against the Sunrise, and with the animals in front of you, pronounce what follows on your knees and bare headed:

"Salt, which is made and formed in the Castle of the Fair, beautiful Saint Elizabeth,[276] in the name of Disolet, Solfée carrying salt, salt, of whose salt, I conjure thee in the Name of Gloria, of Doriante and of Galianne her sister; salt, I conjure thee, that thou mayest aid me to keep hold of my living horses (76) of equine beasts, who are here present before God and before myself, healthy and clean, drinking well, eating well, large and fat, may they in accordance with my wishes. Salt of whose salt, I conjure thee by the power of glory, and by the virtue of glory, and in all my intention always of glory."

With this having been pronounced in the direction of the rising sun, go to the opposite quarter following [the movement of] this Star[277] and there you will pronounce what has been written above. You will do the same at the other quarters and returning to where you began, you will pronounce once more the same words. Make sure that during the ceremony, the animals are always in front of you, because those who are behind or to the side of you, might as well be mad animals.

Afterwards, circle your horses three times, casting pinches of salt over the animals, saying, *"Salt, I cast thee from the hand that God hath given me; Grapin,[278] I take thee, I wait upon thee."* (77)

With the remainder of your salt, you will bleed the animal which is mounted, saying, *"Oh Equine Beast, I bleed thee with the hand that God hath given me; Grapin, I take thee, I wait upon thee."*

It must be bled with a piece of hard wood, such as boxwood or the wood from a pear tree. Draw as much blood as you wish, but some capricious people would say on the matter that certain parts of the animal produce particular virtues. We recommend only that when the blood is drawn, the animal should have its rump away from you. If it is, for example,

---

[275] In the 1670 Edition, this secret is entitled *"Secret to destroy the bewitchment cast upon the animals, in particular horses and sheep"*. There is no reference as to what the Castle of the Fair might refer to. The word Guard might also be translated as *"A Protection Against"*.

[276] St Elizabeth was the sister of the Virgin Mary and the mother of St John the Baptist.

[277] That is to say, clockwise or *deosil*.

[278] Grapin is clearly the name of a being. This might be a corruption of Gryphon, the mythical beast with the body of a lion and head and wings of an eagle.

a sheep, you should hold its head between your legs. Then, after you have bled the animal, collect some of the hoof[279] from the right foot, that is to say that you will cut a piece of the horn from its right foot with a knife, which you split into two pieces and make a cross out of them. You place this little cross into a piece of new cloth, then cover it with your salt. Then take (78) some wool, if you are working on sheep, otherwise, you should take some horsehair, and you should also make a little cross out of it, which you place in your cloth on top of the salt. On top of this wool or horsehair, you put another layer of salt. You then make another small cross from virgin wax used for Easter or a consecrated candle. Then you place the remainder of your salt over it and tie everything into a ball with a piece of string. Rub the animals with this bundle as they leave the stables, if they are horses; if they are sheep, rub them as they come out of the sheepfold or from the sheep pen, pronouncing the words that you will have used for casting the salt. You will continue to rub them for 1, 2, 3, 7, 9 or 11 days in a row. This depends on the strength and vitality of the animals.

Note that you must only throw your salt at the last word. When you are working with the horses, pronounce them swiftly. If it concerns sheep, then it would be better to take your time pronouncing them. If (79) you find a horse hair in the collection of salt to be cast, you must only pronounce them over the salt and not over anywhere else. All of the protections begin on a Tuesday or a Thursday during the waxing of the Moon, and in pressing cases, you can pass over these observations. It is important not to let your bundles become damp, otherwise the animals would perish. Ordinarily, they are to be carried in the gusset,[280] but without charging you with this futile method for caring for them, do as the expert practitioners do: place them in any dry place in your home and you will have nothing to fear. We have said above to take only the horn from the right foot to make the bundle. Most take them from the four feet and consequently make two crosses out of them, since they have four pieces from them. That is superfluous and produces nothing additional. If you do all the ceremonies for the four corners at the single corner of the rising sun, the flock will be less dispersed.

Take note that a wicked shepherd,[281] (80) who resents the person who replaces him, can cause him much grief and can even cause the flock to

---

[279] Lit. *"horn"*.
[280] An insert in the seam of a garment.
[281] In the 1670 Edition, this paragraph is listed as a separate *'secret'*, entitled, *"Another very effective Counter-Charm"*.

perish. Firstly, by means of the bundle, which he cuts into pieces and scatters, either on a table or elsewhere, or through a rosary *Novena*, after which he wraps the bundle with it, then cuts the whole of it and scatters it, either by means of a mole or a weasel, either by the pot or pitch[282] or cruet[283], or finally through means of a common or a green frog, or a cod tail, which they place into an anthill, saying, *"Damnation,*[284] *perdition, etc"*. They leave it there for nine days, after which they lift it out with the same words, grinding it into powder, sowing some of it where the flock is to graze. They also use three pebbles that have been taken from different cemeteries and by means of certain words, which we do not wish to reveal, which give off emanations that cause outbreaks of mange[285] and they cause as many animals to die as they wish. (81) We will give the method for destroying these glamours below, through our methods for breaking the protections and all evil spells. We intend to reprint the *Enchiridion of Pope Leo*[286] on the same subject, in which a good number of mysterious prayers of surprising success can be found. (You should choose the 1740 edition.)

Guard for whatever you will[287]

"Astarin, Astaroth, who is Bahol, I commit my flock to thy charge and thy protection. And for thy salary, I shall give thee a white or a black beast, such as shall please me. I conjure thee, Satarin, that thou mayest guard them for me everywhere in these gardens, while saying, 'Hurlupupin'[288].*"*

You will act in accordance with what we have said in *"The Castle of the Fair"* and cast the salt, pronouncing what follows:

---

[282] The word *"tarc"* is unclear.

[283] All indicating that the pieces are put into food and/or condiments for people to consume and then disperse the pieces through human digestive waste.

[284] Or *"curses"*.

[285] A skin disease caused by parasitic mites.

[286] Pope Leo III is said to have received a document, from Charlemage the Great, in which was a collection of charms in the forms of prayers, that were suppose to give great wealth to the person who made use of them, It also contained charms against perils to the human person, tempests and attacks from wild animals.

[287] In the 1670 Edition, this is called *"Another secret to break a spell"*.

[288] Possibly a *"barbarous"* incantation.

"Gupin, while shoeing, almost has the big one. It is Cain who made it for you."[289]
Rub them using the same words.

Another guard[290]

"Woolly beasts, I take thee[291] *in the name (82) of God and of the most Holy Sacred Virgin Mary. I pray God that the bleeding that I am about to do may take and profit according to my will. I conjure thee that thou mayest break and shatter all spells and enchantments, which may pass over the body of my lively flock of woolly beasts, who are here present before God and before myself, who are under my charge and under my watch. In the name of the Father of the Son and of the Holy Ghost, and of the Lord St John the Baptist and the Lord St Abraham."*

See what we have said above for working with *"The Castle of the Fair"* and you should use the words that follow for the casting and rubbing, *"Passe Flori,*[292] *Jesus is raised from the dead."*

Guard against mange, scabies and sheep-pox[293]

"It was on a Monday in the morning that the saviour of the World passed, the Holy Virgin after him, the Lord St John, his shepherd boy, his friend, who seeketh his divine flock, who is marred by this wicked pox, of which he can take no more, because of the three shepherds (83) who adored my Saviour Redeemer Jesus-Christ in Bethlehem and who have adored the voice of the child."

Say *Pater* and *Ave* five times each.

"My flock shall be healthy and pleasant to look at, which is my issue. I pray to the

---

[289] This sentence is nonsensical and maybe it is intentionally so. The meaning of *"faire cha"* is fairly obscure. I am only guessing at what it could mean in order to make sense. It could be referring to *"faire chanter"*, which would make it mean, *"It is Cain who blackmails you"*, but I don't think so. It could also refer to the Constellation of Caméléon. Most likely *"cha"* is a variant of the pronoun *"ça"*, *"it"*, which makes much more sense and this is how I have translated it.

[290] In the 1670 Edition, this is entitled, *"Against cast lots, another very effective secret"*.

[291] The grammar is inconsistent with linguistic use. Here, *"tu"* should actually be plural *"vous"*, as he is invoking more than one sheep. Unless it is referring to the sheep as a *"collective"*.

[292] Latin: *"Go away, flourish"*.

[293] In the 1670 Edition, this is entitled, *"Guard or Protection against the mange, scabies, sheep pox. and other sicknesses"*.

Lady Saint Genevieve,[294] *that she may serve me as a friend in this, here wicked pox. Pox, banished by God, renounced by J.-C., I command thee by the Great Living God to depart from this place and to melt and be confounded before God and before me, as the dew melts before the Sun. Most Glorious Virgin Mary and Holy Spirit, pox, begone from here, for God commandeth it of thee, as is also true of Joseph, Nicodemus of Arimathea,*[295] *[who] laid down the precious body of my Saviour and Redeemer J.-C., on the day of Good Friday from the Tree of the Cross, of the Father, of the Son, of the Holy Ghost, worthy flock of woolly beasts, come hither, approach God and myself. Behold the divine offering (84) of salt, which I present to thee today. As without salt, nothing hath been done, as I believe it to be, by the Father etc."*

"Oh Salt! I conjure thee by the Great Living God, that thou mayest serve me in that, to which I aspire, that thou mayest preserve me and guard my flock from scabies, mange, growths, from asthma, fragility and from bad waters. I command thee, as commanded Jesus-Christ my Saviour in the boat to his Disciples, when they said to him, "Lord, awake, for the sea doth make us afraid." As soon as the Lord awoke, he commanded the sea to be still. And immediately the sea became calm, commanded by the Father, etc."

Before doing anything in regards to this guard, pronounce over the salt, *"Panem cœlestem accipiat, sit nomen Domine invocabis."*[296] Then referring back to *"The Castle of the Fair"*, do the casting and rubbing, pronouncing that which follows, *"Eum ter [euntes] ergo docentes omnes gentes baptisantes eos. In nomine Patris etc."*[297] (85)

Guard against mange

"When Our-Lord ascended into the Heavens, his holy virtue on Earth left Pasle, Colet and Herve. All that God hath spoken, hath been well spoken. Red, white or black beasts, of whatever colour that thou mayest be, if there be any mange or scabies upon thee, it was placed and made with nine feet in Earth, it is also true that it will walk and will die, as did St John, in its skin and born in its camel,[298] *as Joseph, Nicodemus of*

---

[294] Patron Saint of Paris. Her prayers were said to have saved Paris from attack from Attila the Hun in the 5th century CE.

[295] Joseph of Arimathea is mentioned in all the Gospels as having given his own tomb, laid in preparation for his own burial, to Jesus after his crucifixion.

[296] From the Mass, these words are spoken in the Communion of the Priest. Latin: *"I will take the bread of heaven, and will call upon the name of the Lord."*

[297] Latin: *"Therefore go and make disciples of all nations, baptising them in the name of the Father and of the Son and of the Holy Spirit".* (Matthew 28:19).

[298] This makes little sense but it is what the text says: there is no idiomatic use of the

Arimathea tore down the body of my Saviour Redeemer J.-C. From the tree of the Cross on that day of Good Friday."

You will use the following words for the casting and rubbing and will have referred to what we have said in *"The Castle of the Fair".*

"Oh Salt, I cast thee from the hand that God hath given me. Volo et vono Baptistæ Sancta agalatum est."[299]

Guard for preventing wolves from entering into a field where there are Sheep

Place yourself in the quarter of the rising sun and there pronounce five times what (86) is to follow. If you wish to pronounce it only once, you will do it for as many as five days in a row.

"Come woolly beasts, it is the Lamb of Humility, I protect thee, Ave Maria. It is the Lamb of the Redeemer, who hath fasted for forty days without rebellion, without taking any rest from the enemy, who was tempted in truth. Go straight on, grey beast, with grey claws, so seek thy prey, wolves and she-wolves and wolf cubs, thou may not come to the meat that is here. In the Name of the Father, and of the Son, and of the Holy Ghost and of the fortunate St Cerf.[300] *Begone, Oh Satana!"*

With this having been pronounced in the quarter that we have mentioned, you should continue to do the same at the other quarters. And once you are back to where you started from, it is repeated once more. For the rest, see *"The Castle of the Fair",* then do the casting with the words that follow, *"Vanus vanes Christus vaincus, to the attack Oh salt, soli, to the attack Oh Saint Sylvain*[301] *in the name of Jesus."* (87)

The Marionettes of Protection

"We would go, we would go to them, we would marry and we would marry them, we would untie ourselves and we would marry them to Belzebuth."

---

word *"chameau",* other than to refer to an unpleasant person as a *"chameau"* (camel) in contemporary French.

[299] Corrupted Latin that makes no sense. If *vaincus* was corrupted from *vinculus,* it might have originally meant something like *"Vain and ineffectual to the bond of Christ".*

[300] St Cerf. There is not much information about this saint.

[301] Corrupted Latin that makes no sense. If *vaincus* was corrupted from *vinculus,* it might have originally meant something like *"Vain and ineffectual to the bond of Christ".*

This Guard is dangerous and cumbersome or rather its success is most uncertain. You need the disposition of a most pure soul for it to succeed.

Guard for horses

"Oh Salt, who is made and formed from the foam of the sea, I conjure thee to make my happiness and master's profit. I conjure thee in the name of Crouay,[302] *Don,*[303] *I conjure thee in the name of Crouay. Rou and Rouvayet, come hither, I take thee for my valet.*[304] *Cast! Festi Christi Bélial."*

Make sure to say, *"Rouvayet, that which thou shalt make, shall I find to be well-made."* Because this protection is moreover potent and sometimes tiresome. (88) See what we have instructed in *"The Castle of the Fair"* concerning protections.

Guard for the flock

"Let all beasts of prey,[305]*who would attack this lively flock of woolly beasts be bridled by the "Hoc est enim Corpus meum".*[306] *Woolly beasts, come to me, behold an offering of salt that I present to thee and which I am going to give thee, in the Name of God and of the Virgin and of the Lord St John. Woolly beasts, come to me and turn towards me. Behold an offering of blessed salt from God, which I will give thee, deliver and cast, in the name of God, of the Virgin and of the Lord St John. Woolly beasts, come to me, behold an offering of salt blessed by God, which I present to thee and am going to deliver and cast over thee. Lively flock of woolly beasts, which is here present before God and before myself, in the Name of God and of the Virgin, and of the Lord St. John, may this salt protect them for me, to be healthy and clean, well-watered, well-fed, (89) fat and large, base and lowly, close and enclosed around myself, as is the lamb of St John. And to his honour, I believe that this salt will guard them for me, to be healthy and clean,*

---

[302] EL: Crouay -> Croix.

[303] Interestingly, a Brithonic word (Welsh and Breton) that relates to the sea. In Welsh, it is a *'wave'* and in Breton, it refers to the *'depths'*.

[304] As the *'l'* sound was sometimes assimilated into an *'ou'* sound, it is possible that these names may be a corruption of the name of Rollo to Rou. Rollo (846-931 CE) was the king who founded the principality of Normandy. This could then indicate that Rouvayet is a corruption of Rollo's valet (as valet is later in the line), and the phrase was originally *'Rollo and Rollo's valet'*.

[305] In the 1670 Edition, this reads as, *"All beasts, who would attack this lively flock of woolly beasts..."*

[306] Latin: *"This is my body"*. The words the Priest pronounces over the wafer/bread at the Eucharist, when the bread or wafer is transubstantiated into the body of Christ.

well-watered and well-fed, large and fat, as the lamb of the Lord St. John. I believe that this salt will guard them for me, to be bright and shiny, to be pleasing to the whole world, in the name of God and of the Virgin and of the Lord St. John. I believe that this salt will protect them from wolves and she-wolves and from all manner of marauding beasts, who prowl both day and night. Oh blessèd salt of God, I conjure thee that thou mayest grant me this; for I believe in it, in the name of God, of the Virgin and of the Lord St. John. Oh great God, I believe that this salt will preserve them for me from scabies, from mange, from sheep-pox and from any ill that may overcome the body of this lively flock of woolly beasts. Oh blessèd salt of God, I believe that thou wilt grant me this in the name of God and of the Virgin and of the Lord St. John. Amen."

You should say a *Mass of the Holy Spirit* (90) over the salt. It must be started with the *"Confiteor"*[307] and continued until the end. You may say it yourself. For the remainder, you will thereby proceed as in *"The Castle of the Fair"* and you will use the following words for the casting, etc.

"Vamus Jesus Christus et memores,[308] attack sullied salt, attack Oh St Sylvain[309] in the name of Jesus."

Another Guard[310] for sheep

"Oh salt, who hath been made by God and blessed by his most worthy man, I conjure thee by the Great Living God and by the Lord St Riquier,[311] who is the fighter of all Devils, I conjure thee that thou mayest break and corrupt all words that have been spoken, read and celebrated over the body of this lively flock of woolly beasts, that are here present before God and before myself. Oh salt, who hath been created by God and blessed by his worthy hand, I conjure, present and apply [thee] over the body of this lively flock, that are here present before God and before myself, it is my intention and my desire, that thou (91) mayest guard them for me, to be healthy and clean, large and fat and round, that they may be well united around myself, as the belt of the Most Holy Virgin

---

[307] This is the general confession of sin that is recited at the beginning of the Mass.
[308] If *vamus* was a corruption of *varius*, this might roughly be translated from the Latin as: *"Manifold Jesus Christ and remember"*. Pissier suggests, *"Jesus Christ is powerless and [men] are mindful"* (2011:79).
[309] Very little is known about St Silvan, except that he was a martyred saint from the fourth century and his body lies in an incorruptible state in the Church of St. Blaise in Dubrovnik, Croatia. Salt is known as a preservative, as this is why St Silvan may have been invoked here on account of his *"preserved"* body.
[310] Or *"protection"*, according to the 1670 Edition.
[311] This is the French for Richarius, a Frankish monk who founded two monasteries in the 7th century CE, who is still venerated by the Catholic Church.

Mary, when she was carrying the body of my sweet Saviour and Redeemer J.-C.. Casta sacravera viga corpus Domini nostri Jesus Christi qui tima menta Deus; in nomine Patri, et Filii, et Spiritus Sancti. Amen.'[312]

For its application, refer to what is taught in *"The Castle of the Fair"* and for the casting and the rubbing use the words that follow, or those for the castings above, as suits you, *"Passe Flori, Jesus is risen from the dead!"*

New Guard for sheep, taught by the learnèd Bellerot, in his treatise on the preservation of woolly beasts.

Procure a church candle which will have been used for the first Easter-tide communion of a young girl born to wise and virtuous parents. Light it and place it into the earth, not far from a river or a stream, where you will lead (92) your sheep to pasture. Trace a big semi-circle capable of enclosing your flock and for that, use a mystical wand, whose composition is indicated in the *Veritable Red Dragon* on page 18 (*Black Hen* Edition).[313] This being done, sit on a layer of earth, which you will have arranged beforehand and after you have commended yourself to the Most Holy Trinity, you will make the three appeals marked in the *Red Dragon* on page 30 and onwards, taking care to have the mystical wand in your hand always, which has just been mentioned in order to carry out its indicated use.[314]

The spirit will appear to you and you will command him to touch each one of the sheep present and to commit him, or one of his subordinates, now and forever to the protection of your flock, which he will do at that very instance. (See the figure at the beginning of this volume).

What we have given in way of protections, must suffice to satisfy the (93) shepherd and the sheep-breeder, since one protection which can serve for one, can serve for another changing only the name of the *"lively flock of woolly beasts"* to *"equine beasts"*. In each case, it is good to note that the stronger and more replete with ingratiation a protection is, the better it will serve for horses and the sweeter and more sound the protection is, the better it will serve for sheep. And so that the labourer may draw particular fruit from our discoveries, we are going to follow with a protection which

---

[312] Again corrupted, but the Latin reads something like: *"The Pure and Most Sacred Living Body of our Lord Jesus Christ, who by mental fear of God, in the name of the Father and of the Son and of the Holy Spirit."*

[313] The *Veritable Red Dragon* was the same book as *the Grand Grimoire*.

[314] That is the three conjurations of Lucifer in that work.

concerns him particularly. It is of an infinite resource for those who are near rabbit warrens or near other areas where there are rabbits. The animals will not be able to harm the harvest, as long as you observe what we are going to teach. When they come upon the grains that need to be protected, they will, on the contrary, destroy the weeds there.

Guard against rabbits

Put some salt on a plate or on a tray: the quantity may not need be (94) fixed, that depends on the extent of the land, which you wish to protect. In addition, have some rabbit droppings and five pieces of tiles, collected from a Procession in a cemetery. Then being at the location where you wish to carry out this operation, you will commence from the side of the rising sun, with a bare head and on your knees. You will say what follows and will make crosses on the salt: "✝ *dant* ✝ *dant* ✝ *dant sant* ✝ *Heliot and Valiot.*[315] *Rouvayet come hither and I take thee for my valet, to guard here against these cursed bucks and doe, that they may pass through and pass across this field of (name the grain), which is here present before God and before myself, without doing any harm nor damage, may they be bridled on behalf of Réveillot. For I command thee and conjure thee on behalf of the Great Living God, to obey me, thee and thy comrades, to do what I am going to ask of thee, which is to guard for three months and three Moons, this field of N., which is here present before God (95) and before myself, as thus I believe by the faith that I have in thee. Thus, I believe that thou wilt do it. Thus I believe it by the virtue of this salt blessed by God and by the virtue of the little pieces of tile and droppings of the said bucks and doe. Thus do I believe by all the forces and powers that thou mayest have over them. Thus do I believe.*"

Make a hole in the earth, place one rabbit dropping into it, saying, *"Rou and Rouvayet, come hither, I take thee for my valet."*

Place a pinch of salt onto the dropping, saying, *"Salt, I do place thee, by the hand that God hath given me, Rou and Rouvayet, come hither, I take thee for my valet."*

Then place a piece of tile, saying, *"Piece of tile, I place thee by the hand that God hath given me."*

Tap the piece of tile with your left heel, turning to the right and saying, *"Rou and Rouvayet, come hither, I take thee for my valet."*

This is also done at the three other corners, then cross to the middle

---

[315] EL: Valiot -> Vajoith?.

(96) of the field, where what has been done at one of the corners is then done at this middle piece. Return to the first corner and there begin your castings. At the first [corner], you say, *"Salt, I cast thee from the hand that God hath given me, anchor to the Virgin."* Being back at the place from which you started, take the rest of your salt and cast it with one sole throw, saying, *"Rou and Rouvayet, come hither, I take thee for my valet."*

If the land is divided into different plots of different grains, the same ceremonies need to be done for each plot. In place of three months and three Moons, you will name what you please.

We can find other varieties of protections in the *Magical Works of Agrippa*, printed in Rome in 1744 and where you can also find the secret of *The Queen of Hairy Flies*.

To stop horses and carriages[316]

On black paper, trace with (97) white ink, the pentacle figured on the title cover of this book, printed in 1760. Throw this pentacle thus traced at the horses' heads and say:

"White or black horse, of whatever colour that thou mayest be, it is I who maketh thee do it, I conjure thee that thou mayest not pull any more with thy feet as thou dost with thy ears, no more may Beelzebuth break thy chain."

For this operation, a nail forged during Midnight Mass is necessary, which you drive in the place, where the harness passes. Lacking this, a scab[317] is taken and is conjured as follows:

"Scab, I conjure thee in the name of Lucifer, Beelzebuth and of Satanas, the three princes of all the devils, that thou stop thyself."

For three days before the day you wish to perform this operation, you should be careful not to do any Christian work.

Counter-Charm

"Hostia sacra verra corrum,[318] *while repelling the Great Devil of Hell, (98) all*

---

[316] According to the 1670 Edition, this *'secret'* is about taming wild horses, not about stopping horses and carriages. Its title reads, *"To tame malicious horses"*.
[317] This word could alternatively mean *'drake'*, but it seems more likely that a scab could be secreted on the harness than a male duck!
[318] Again barbarous Latin, but perhaps: *"Destroyed by the true holy sacrifice"*.

words, enchantments and characters that have been said, read and celebrated over the body of my lively horses, may they be broken and shattered behind me." After that, you conclude with the prayer that begins with these words, *"Word, which hath become flesh, etc"* and which you will find in the *Enchiridion Léonis Papæ*,[319] from the 1740 edition.

For the lambs to return[320] beautiful and very strong

Take the first-born; failing that, take the first to come to you. Lift it up from the ground with its nose towards you, then say:

"Ecce lignum crucem in quo salus mundi crucem"[321]

Place it back down, lift it up again and say as above. Do the same three times. With that done, you will pronounce the Prayer of the Day for current day in a low voice, and which is found written in the *Enchiridion of Pope Leo.*

Against firearms[322]

"Star, which leads the weapon today, thee whose barrel[323] I do charm, to thee I say, (99) obey me. In the name of the Father and of the Son and Sanatatis."[324] Make The Sign of the Cross. Also see pages 53 and 57.

For ulcerous lesions[325]

Take the first sheep that comes to you afflicted with the said illness. Having turned towards the direction of the rising sun, with its mouth opened, you pronounce into it the words that follow three times:

---

[319] *The Enchiridion of Pope Leo.* See note 270 above.
[320] Lit *"to come back".* In the other editions (1670 and 1800), the word used is *"deviennent"* - *"become",* which would also make sense.
[321] Behold the wood of the cross on which the Saviour of the world was crucified. A corruption of the Latin phrase used in the Good Friday liturgy, *"Ecce lignum crucis, in quo salus mundi pependit",* *"Behold the wood of the cross on which hung the Saviour of the world."*
[322] In the 1670 Edition, this is entitled, *"protection against all firearms".*
[323] The word *Gige* maybe a misspelling of *"gigue",* which sometimes refers to a *"long leg",* here it might refer to the barrel of the gun. The language of this passage is quite obscure.
[324] Possibly a copying error, as in the other edition, it is given as *"Satanatis".*
[325] Literally, *"clumps".*

"Brac, Cabrac Carabra, Cadebrac, Cabracam, I heal thee."[326]

Each time, blow into the mouth of the sheep and cast it amongst the others. They will all be healed. As many Signs of the Cross need to be done as there are sheep with lesions on them.

For glanders[327] and colic in horses[328]

"(name the [colour of the] hair) Horse, belonging to N., if thou hast glanders, of whatever colour that they be, and abdominal cramps or renal colic or of thirty six kinds of other ills, whatever case they may be, may God and also the blessèd Saint Eligius[329] heal thee: (100) in the name of the Father and of the Son and of the Holy Ghost." Then say the *Pater* five times and the *Ave* etc. five times, on your knees.

As soon as you have pronounced these words, if the horse has glanders, you should inject the following decoction into its throat with a syringe:

Take a handful of flowers from the elder tree[330] and some camomile. Simmer them in two pints of water, filter everything and add to it half an ounce of ammonia salt,[331] three ounces of anti-scorbutic syrup[332] and half a pint of vinegar.[333] Reiterate the words and the injections several times during the day.

If it is afflicted with abdominal cramps, in place of the remedy above, employ the following:

---

[326] These words seem to be derived from the reduction charm based on Abracadabra, which was written repeatedly and reduced by a letter on each line, so it ended with just the letter a.

[327] This is a contagious disease chiefly of horses and mules but communicable to humans, caused by the bacterium *Pseudomonas mallei* and characterized by swellings beneath the jaw and a profuse mucous discharge from the nostrils.

[328] In the 1670 Edition, this is just called *"Against all manner of sicknesses in horses"*.

[329] Saint Eligius, otherwise known as Saint Éloi in French, born in the 6th century CE in *Aquitaine* in France, is the patron saint of all persons who work with metals, including goldsmiths. He is also the patron saint of coin collectors. He is also known as the patron saint of horses.

[330] Elder was known to reduce inflammation and camomile is known for its soothing properties.

[331] *Ammonium chloride*: used medicinally as an expectorant in cough medicines, also to induce vomiting, as well as for urinary tract disorders.

[332] Usually extracted juices of citrus fruits, to prevent scurvy.

[333] *Vinegar* was used for a variety of medical uses, amongst which was its use as an anti-microbial

After bleeding the horse, make him swallow a pound of olive oil[334] and give it some linseed enemas.[335]

To heal sprains and twists in horses[336]

"Atay de satay suratay avalde,[337] (101) *walk!"* It should be repeated three times, striking the hoof of the horse. If it is on the side of the saddle, then strike the left foot.

At the same time, apply a vinegar compress around the fetlock, in which you will have steeped some sage and some rosemary.[338] This compress should be renewed each time that it cools down. You would do well to also bleed the animal at its neck.

To prevent a flock from touching the grain, passing between two furrows[339]

Take a piece of silver, hang it from the neck of one of the sheep, saying what follows nine times:

"Satan, Satourne, speaker of Gricacœur da voluptere Seigneur de Nazariau,[340] *I request and command thee and humbly conjure thee to come to guard and pass the evening, the day and the morning with my lively flock of woolly beasts, while saying hurlupupin."*[341]

We do not wish to say anything more about these words of ingratiation. (102)

---

[334] Although *olive oil* was usually used as a medium to deliver other herbs into a person or animal through ingestion, it was also known to be effective to block intestinal contractions and effective against Borborygmus.

[335] Linseed is known to possess anti-inflammatory properties.

[336] In the 1670 Edition, this secret also heals twists and sprains in humans: *"To heal sprains and twists in men and in animals"*.

[337] More unknown words, note however the rhyming nature of the charm.

[338] *Sage* was often used as a local anaesthetic when applied on the skin. Rosemary, it is said, revitalises paralysed limbs and treats gout.

[339] In the 1670 Edition, this is entitled, *"to prevent a flock from touching a harvest"*.

[340] French, roughly, *"The Greek heart of the pleasure of the lord of Nazareth"*.

[341] See note on page 81 of the text.

To heal a beast afflicted with haemorrhaging

Take the afflicted beast and say the words that follow three times over its head:

"In tes dalame bouis, vins Divernas Satan."[342]

For mumps[343]

Take some holy water and with the end of your finger and touching beneath your jaws, say:

" ✝ Christus brutus et datus et vanum"[344]

For scabies and ringworm[345] in animals

"Gupin while shoeing almost has the big one. It is Cain who made it for you"[346] Take some flowers of sulphur[347] with oil and a pinch of salt, make an ointment from it, which you will rub with animals with, while pronouncing the words above: Repeat until healed.[348]

---

[342] *"Sathan"* in the 1670 Edition. The sentence is nonsensical and corrupt Latin, with an element of Occitan.

[343] This is an educated guess, as *"godron"* translates as *"gadroon"*. It is obviously a sickness. It may well refer to *"mumps"*, as the swollen glands can be shaped like bowls (gadroons are the ornaments around the tops of bell shaped vessels) and the visible swelling from mumps occurs in the parotid glands, which is found under the jaw.

[344] Corrupted Latin: *"Christ, is stupid and handed over (or given) and is useless"*. Perhaps originally the phrase would have translated as something like *'Christ I give you this stupid and empty [illness]'*.

[345] The translation for *"haut toupin"* is an educated guess and probably refers to a skin disease in animals. It could possibly refer to a *"tick"* infestation.

[346] See note on page 81. The only variation here is that version reads *"Gupin"*, while elsewhere it reads *"Lupin"*.

[347] *Amorphous sulphur* in a fine powder. It was often used medicinally to treat skin ailments. It was also used as a fungicide, which supports the translation of *"ringworm"*.

[348] The formula is very different in the 1670 Edition. It reads, *"Take some wheat flour, some oil, a pinch of salt and some blood drawn from three animals. Knead everything and make a flat cake out of it. Wrap it in paper and cook it over hot embers, rub the animals with it, pronouncing the words above."*

For hæmorrhoids[349]

With the finger of the middle hand, [take] some saliva from your mouth and touch the hæmorrhoids, saying:

"Piles, begone, God curseth thee. (103) *In the name of the Father and of the Son and of the Holy Ghost."*

After this, say the *Pater* and *Ave* nine times for nine days. On the second day, you only say them eight times and you reduce the number of times each day in order.

Two times in a day, you should rub the hæmorrhoids with some fresh butter in which you will have cooked some inner bark from the elder tree.[350]

For epilepsy or falling sickness

Place the epileptic in a well-aired placed, rub his forearms and say into his right ear:

"Oremus præceptis salutaris moniti."[351]

Add the *Dominican Prayer.*[352] Before these prayers have been completed, the sick man will rise up again.

An excellent remedy against the falling sickness, is sap ensuing from an incision made in a lime-tree[353] in the month of February. Each time, it is given in three ounce quantities.

END

---

[349] A simplified version of this charm is found in the *Enchiridion* of Pope Leo III. It is also found in *Les Oeuvres Magiques d'Henri Corneille Agrippa*, 1744:99.
[350] The *Elder Tree* and its fruit are better known for treating respiratory infections, rather than hæmorrhoids.
[351] Latin: *"Let us pray. Admonished by salutary precepts."* From the Traditional Latin Mass.
[352] Prayed on the Rosary.
[353] The *Lime tree* or *Tilia*, was used as a nervine, used for restlessness and hysteria. It was commonly thought that sitting under Lime Trees could cure epilepsy in folklore, as its scent was quite heady and intoxicating.

(108) **SOME MORE PRECIOUS ADDITIONS**

We have thought that it would add to this volume's merit by completing it with the reproduction of some secrets that were in the possession of a family that was set apart by its piety. We believe that we can affirm that many people have benefited from having made use of them. (109)

FAMILY REMEDIES

For Dropsy[354]

Take a handful of the plant called *Queen of the Meadow*.[355] Infuse it in a pint of boiling water. Make a fervent prayer to Saint Eutrope,[356] first bishop of Saintes, then drink three glasses of this infusion three times, one in the morning, one at midday and one in the evening, one hour before eating. Repeat each day and for fifteen or so [minutes], do your prayer before drinking and you will inevitably be healed.

For Cuts

When a large vein has not been affected, let the cut run a little in order to clear the smaller veins which will be surrounding the cut.

With this done, wash with some fresh water, while saying a *Pater* and an *Ave* (110) in honour of St Anthony[357] and St Isabelle,[358] then place a spider's

---

[354] *Œdema*. Also known as *hydropsy*. Accumulation of fluid under the skin, usually in the lower legs, often associated with either cardiac failure or kidney disease.

[355] *Filipendula ulmaria*. Also known as *meadowsweet*. It has diuretic properties, which no doubt is why it is used here to help drain the subcutaneous fluid.

[356] St Eutropius of *Saintes*. He was the first Bishop of *Saintes* (a French commune located in *Poitou-Charentes*) in the first century CE. He was martyred after he converted a Pagan Roman governor's daughter, *Eustelle* to Christianity.

[357] St Antoine: St Anthony or Anthony the Great was an Egyptian Saint in the 2nd-3rd century CE. Although he was considered to be the first ascetic he was erroneously thought to have been the first monk. However, his biography by St Athanasius of Alexandria helped to spread monasticism. St Anthony was often called upon to help with afflictions and diseases of the skin.

[358] St Isabelle of France: Died 1270, was the daughter of Louis VIII of France. She was known for her piety and refusal to marry her suitors, many of noble families and founded the Franciscan Abbey of *Longchamp*, west of Paris. Although she did not wish to become the abbess, she lived out her life in austerity and was known to minister to the sick and poor.

web[359] or tinder fungus[360] over it, or even two,[361] purged of all bits of straw.

When the hæmorrhage has been stemmed, wash with tepid water mixed with a little good quality *eau-de-vie*,[362] bring the fleshy sides of the cut together and place a leaf of valerian[363] over it, wrapped with some linen and be certain of the healing.

For Iron Splinters That Have Entered Into The Eyes

If it happens that you get an iron splinter in your eyes or one of these little grains of iron originating from iron filings, which is common with blacksmiths and locksmiths, do what you can not to move, nor close and open the eyes before having pronounced or have pronounced by a person who is at hand close to you, the following prayer, addressed to St Claire,[364] Virgin, whose festival is celebrated on the 12th August:

"Blessèd Saint Claire, who died in (111) sentiments of piety that were so pure and so sincere that God wished for you to be canonised, so that by your efficacious intercession, I may obtain prompt healing of the ills that I do endure."

During this prayer, you will procure a strong magnet and you will get someone to hold your eyelids open, while another person holds the magnet as close as is possible to your eye.

If your prayer to Saint Claire has been fervent, this method will succeed without any doubt. If you are lacking a magnet, roll a piece of white paper in such a way that one side forms a point, so that the person can guide the

---

[359] It was thought that cobwebs helped stem the flow of blood from a wound and promoted healing.

[360] *Fomes fomentarius*: a bracket fungus, sometimes known as *Amadou*, originally used as tinder for starting fires. It was used in medicine as an anti-hæmorragic (to stop bleeding).

[361] Fibres of hemp, flax or jute used in the textile industry to make fibres for upholstery.

[362] Lit. Brandy. Since *eau-de-vie* has been adopted as an English word for a distilled alcoholic beverage made from a fruit other than the grape, it is fit to use it instead of the more common term *'brandy'*.

[363] *Valeriana officinalis*. *Valerian* is better known for its sedative properties in assisting sleeping disorders.

[364] St Claire (or Clare) of Assisi, died in 1253. She was one of the first followers of St Francis of Assisi. She is thought to be the first woman who wrote down monastic rules. She is also known to have founded the *"Order of Poor Ladies"*, which was a monastic religious order for women in the Franciscan tradition.

splinter or the iron filing with this point gently towards the corner of the eye and remove it.

For White Finger[365]

Everyone knows how painful this illness is and how dangerous it is if you don't treat it immediately and clear it up. (112)

As soon as you notice that the base of the finger[nail] is swollen and inflamed, you need to take one egg yolk, beat it with half a pinch of salt, covering the affected part by means of a linen cloth folded double several times over, on to which the egg yolk that has thus been prepared is spread and fixed in place with a cloth band, bound over the tumour.

With this done, take a white cockerel, consecrate it to St Peter and offer it to him with a fervent prayer, demanding relief from him. Twenty four hours later, if your prayer has been heard, at the base of the finger[nail]and close to the nail, a little clot filled with water will have formed, which you should pierce; you will receive relief and healing will follow not long after.

You must preserve the white cockerel, which must neither be killed nor sold, if you wish to avoid the return of your sickness.

For hæmorrhages and blood loss

All pious persons may (113) call upon Saint Raymond of Pégnafort[366] when they are struck with hæmorrhaging and often their prayers are crowned with complete success.

But as nothing good can happen without Faith,[367] it appears that several

---

[365] This probably refers to the diseases known as either Whitlow or *Paronychia*, which are infections of the finger and fingernail. It is unlikely to refer to *Reynaud's Syndrome*, where the fingers turn white, since the text specifically refers to an infection, which is not usually present in *Raynaud's Syndrome*.

[366] Born in Spain in 1175 CE and died at the age of 99. It is said that not wanting to be surprised by the unexpected arrival of the Lord, he spent the last 35 years of his life preparing for his death. One of the miracles he was known for, was to visit 53 places by sea, using only his cloak as a sailing vessel. There is a stained glass representation of him in the Chapel of St Aquilin in the Cathedral of *Évreux* in Normandy, Northern France.

[367] The word *"Faith"* capitalised may refer to faith that St Raymond's companion lacked when he was invited to sail with him on the saint's cloak. Preferring the assured security of the harbour, he declined to set sail with St Raymond on his outer

persons have not had their prayers granted. So for those people, they are better suited to receive material[368] remedies. We are going to present the ones that have until now been effective.

Where a nose bleed is concerned, you should not stop it, unless it lasts for too long. There exist several methods in order to stem it. The first consists of inserting a small amount of lint soaked in a little alum[369] water into the nostrils. [In] the second, you want to breathe in [the fumes of] vinegar mixed with water, while at the same time applying compresses soaked with the same mixture onto the temples. The third and the easiest is to apply a medium-weighted key onto the back between the scapulæ.[370] (114)

For internal hæmorrhages, which are the most dangerous of all, if you do not have the possibility of calling upon the advice of a doctor immediately, you should take pills of alum, the size of a pea, one every two hours.

For Relentless Diarrhœa

Boil eight to ten leaves of plantain[371] in a half litre of milk, strain it and sweeten it. To be taken hot, in three doses one hour apart in the morning and whilst fasting.[372] The diarrhœa often ceases on the first day. It is, however, acceptable to continue to use it for a few more days.

Lime water[373] is also most favourable for this same affliction and gravity. The dose is three half glasses a day, diluted with an equal part of milk and sweetened. That is to say, one in the morning, one at midday and one in the evening.

---

garment.

[368] As in medicinal, rather than spiritual.

[369] *Hydrated potassium aluminium sulphate* otherwise known as *"potassium alum"*. It is used in folk medicine to disinfect wounds and to stem blood flows.

[370] Or *"shoulder blades"*.

[371] This would refer to the *Plantago* plant rather than Plantain Bananas. We usually refer to the *Plantago* plant by its other name, *Psyllium*, which is a well-known remedy for addressing gastric complaints and discomforts.

[372] That is to say, *"on an empty stomach"*.

[373] *Saturated calcium hydroxide* solution. In medicine it is used as an antacid and absorbs carbon dioxide to prevent carbon dioxide poisoning. It was also used for babies' *"gripes"* and other digestive ailments, including nausea and vomiting. When added to milk (to provide nourishment) it was also used to treat diarrhoea.

OBSERVATION: by consulting the information given on the following page, you should be able to avoid some frequent and ghastly[374] errors. (115)

CORRESPONDENCES OF ANCIENT WEIGHTS WITH DECIMAL WEIGHTS

The ancient pound is worth................................500 grams

The ounce..32-

The gros[375]...4-

The grain[376]..0.5 centigrams[377]

The litre..1 kilogram

The demi-litre or chopine[378].............................500 grams

The quarter of a litre[379] or demi-setier[380]............250-

The glass or the glass-full...............................100 to 125 grams

The dessert-spoon[381]....................................15-

The teaspoon..4-

The drop..0.5 centigrams

---

[374] Lit. *"cruel"*.

[375] A *gros* was an ancient unit of weight, worth 3 *deniers* (an ancient monetary system) or1/64th of a pound or 3.8 grams.

[376] And ancient unit or weight used in France. 24 *grains* made a *scrupule*, which weighed roughly 1.27 grams. One *gros* equalled 3 *scrupules*.

[377] One *centigram* is a 100th of a gram.

[378] A *chopine* nowadays refers to *"half a glass of wine"*. It was historically used to define half a pint.

[379] The text has *"titre"* but I am pretty sure that this is a typo and it should be a *"litre"*. There is a word *"titre"* but it refers to a chemical component of a solution.

[380] A *setier* derives from the Latin word *sextarius,* which means a sixth part of. It had different measurements in different parts of France and could not be thought of as a standard unit of measurement. It was sometimes used to denote a Parisian *chopine,* which was equivalent to 24 cubic inches.

[381] This refers to British and British Commonwealth usage of the word. In the USA (and in some parts of Canada), the measurement would be called a *"tablespoon"*. A dessert-spoon refers to a soup spoon in American English, whereas a tablespoon in British and British Commonwealth usage would refer to a serving spoon in American English.

A handful: This is what can be held in the hand. It is the equivalent to 200 or 300 grams. This is how inactive plant substances are prescribed.

A pinch: This is what you can take between your thumb and your index finger. It corresponds to a few grams. (116)

TABLE OF MEDICATION DOSES

Medication doses are usually prescribed for a 24 hour period.

According to Gaubius,[382] the dose of any medication to an adult being 1, will [accordingly] be per person:

From 1 years old	: 1/15 to 1/12	From 7 years old	: 1/3
2	: 1/8	14	: 1/2
3	: 1/6	20	: 2/3
4	: 1/4	20 to 60	: 1

The doses are generally weaker for women than they are for men, [and also for] old people of 75 to 80 years of age.

The doses that we indicate in the Health [section] are those for adults. (117)

OTHER ADDITIONS

We will add to the previous Family Secrets, those that we have been able to gather through means of incessant research, but those which we wanted to impart to you are not accompanied by pious recommendations. In order to compensate for [such] a regrettable omission, we will entreat our readers to ask their Patron Saint or the Holy Virgin to agree to intercede before God to certify that the remedies, of which they may wish to make use, will be as efficacious as they desire.... The prayer may not always be granted, but it will never make a sick man's situation worse and in every case, it may strengthen his patience and double his courage through hope.

---

[382] Hieronymus David Gaubius (1705–1780) was a German physician and chemist from Heidelberg, Germany. He was best known for his work *Institutiones Pathologiae medicinalis*, which was a 1758 treatise on systematic pathology.

Remedy For Gout

Every evening before retiring, three hours after a light (118) meal, take a foot-bath from an extended decoction of flowers from the ash tree[383] and the elder tree[384] (a handful of each). This remedy promptly alleviates pains.

Remedy For Bee-stings

The juice from honeysuckle berries[385] makes the pain and swelling caused by bee-stings cease instantly. It would therefore be prudent to plant honeysuckle in the proximity of beehives.

For Colic

Boil a great big handful of mullein[386] in some milk in order to make a plaster out if it, which you will then apply over the stomach of the sick person. Make it as hot as he can tolerate. Ordinarily, the patient will not delay in falling asleep and he will find himself to be healed when he wakes.

For Cholera

This has been used to great success on various occasions by (119) the inhabitants of the district of Lorient[387] (Morbihan).

It consists of nothing more than [drinking] a bowl of sweetened milk, into which a small glassful of olive oil and a small glassful of eau-de-vie are mixed.

You should go to bed and cover yourself well and it will not be long before you perspire profusely; it is this action that causes the healing.

---

[383] *Fraxinus*: not to be confused with the Mountain Ash or Rowan tree. Its flowers were usually used as a mild laxative. Gout is usually treated with the leaves from Ash trees rather than its flowers.

[384] *Sambucus nigra*: can be used for sprains, bruises and external wounds.

[385] *Lonicera*: honeysuckle and also known as woodbine was an ancient remedy for urinary problems and for asthma. However, it is well known for giving relief from bee-stings in herbal medicine.

[386] Verbascum: of which there are at least 250 flowering varieties. Its usual medicinal use is in treating respiratory complaints, such as coughs and asthma.

[387] A town off the south coast of Brittany, a region of North West France. *Morbihan* is the name of the *Département*, in which *Lorient* is located.

For Jaundice

This sickness can be cured in three or four days, by drinking a pint of sweetened infusion made from carrots,[388] rupturewort[389] and elderflower every day.

For Toothache

Inhale some *eau-de-vie* placed in the hollow of your hand several times and sniff it with the nostril on the side of the rotten tooth, which produces a metastasis,[390] which results in the immediate cessation of the pain. (120)

For Sea Sickness

An old traveller, who has travelled through all the lands of the globe has shown us a protection, with which he has had much experience, not for himself, as he had no need for it, but for persons of a delicate and nervous disposition.

This protection is most simple to prepare. It involves procuring for yourself a good handful of sea salt. In order to purge it of all moisture, throw it into a pan and dry fry it over a gentle fire. When the salt is perfectly dry, let it cool down and spread it out in a sachet made of muslin or fine cloth, the size of the length and breadth of the hand. This sachet is placed on the pit of the stomach at the moment of embarkation.

Recipes For Prolonging Life

The following methods for extending[391] existence have been passed on to the Count Stanislas Kossakowski[392] by centenarians, who have used them.

---

[388] *Daucus carota subsp. Sativus*, the carrot is actually a proven remedy for jaundice.
[389] *Herniaria*: once used as a herbal remedy for hernias. It can also be used as a diuretic.
[390] *"Metastasis"* usually refers to the process of a disease spreading, but here, it refers to the effect of the nostril expanding through the fumes of the brandy.
[391] Lit *"pushing back"*.
[392] Not much is known about the Count Stanislas Kossakowski. It seems that he wrote a comedy play called *Tristan de la Rêverie* (Tristan of the *Rêverie*) published in Paris by Dentu in 1838. But he was also the author of a work entitled Essay of Practical Medicine, including a few ideas on the aetiology of diseases from the point of view of treatment and a collection of popular recipes, published by J.-B. Baillière

It is known that the countries of the North are those where old age is reached the slowest.[393] (121)

I.   Infusion or decoction of ash tree leaves, taken in the morning in place of tea. The centenarian who took this decoction every day had been full of gout at fifty years old. We have already spoken about the use of ash tree leaves for chronic rheumatism and gout manifold times. The experience of others demonstrates that the leaves keep the stomach clear, which is a good remedy for preventing congestion in old people. The dose is 8 grams of leaves per litre of water.

Brush your stomach, morning and night and then brush your feet with a fairly hard brush.

(Passed on by a centenarian soldier)

Every morning, take a decoction of angelica root.[394]

(Passed on by a man of the people who was more than a 100 years old)

Take a small glass of the decoction made from buckbean[395] every day.

(Passed on by an old centenarian lady) (122)

The buckbean or Menyanthes is one of our best indigenous bitters.[396] The dose is 4 to 8 grams to a demi-litre of boiling water. You should leave it infuse until it cools right down.

For Sweaty Feet

Wipe your feet with a dry piece of linen, when you get out of bed and when they are sweaty again, wipe a little sponge soaked in eau-de-vie over them.

---

et fils, Paris in1858, which is probably the source of these recipes.

[393] This is not the literal translation, which would be, *"where one reaches old age the most distant"* but I have given the idea, that old age is achieved after a long period of time.

[394] There are about 60 species in this genus of plant.

[395] *Menyanthes*: Known as the *Buckbean* or *Bog-bean*. An aquatic herb. The literal translation is Water Clover, but this is a different plant altogether.

[396] Considered to be digestives, alcoholic beverages infused with a herb to help the digestion of food.

ESSENTIAL ADVICE

We recommend to lovers[397] of supernatural sciences to read the following works here-below. They will be able to gain some great advantages from them.

The Admirable Secrets of Albert Magnus.

The Veritable Red Dragon (the edition with *The Black Pullet*).

The Enchiridion (sic) of Pope Leo[398] (the Rome 1720 edition).

The Veritable Black Magic, printed in 1750[399] (123)

The Magical Works of Henri Cornelius Agrippa, in which is found *The Secret of the Queen of the Hairy Flies.*

The Wondrous Secrets of Natural Magic of Petit Albert

Treasure of the Old Man of the Pyramids, veritable science of talismans, with *The Black Owl,* a fabulous bird, which uncovers all the precious things that the earth hides.

Little Secret of the Divinatory Wand, to find the most hidden of things.

The Red Magic,[400] cream of occult and natural or divinatory sciences.

The Future Revealed, or Astrology, or The Study of Horoscopes and the ancient divination arts explained by the Seers of the Middle Age.

The Elements of Chiromancy, or the Art of Explaining the future by the lines and signs of the hand.

A Complete Manual of Dæmonology, or the tricks of Hell uncovered.

Phylacteries[401] or protections against diseases, curses and enchantments, exorcisms or conjurations, etc, etc.

---

[397] Lit. *"amateurs"* but the French probably refers to fans of Occult Sciences rather than hacks.

[398] This should be the *Enchiridion* of Pope Leo, but it is misspelt in the French text. It may well be a typo of the transcriber. *Enchiridion* comes from Greek, meaning *"a handbook"* or *"a small manual"*.

[399] Based on the date, this is likely to be the *Grand Grimoire*, which mentions Black Magic in its subtitle.

[400] There are no clear references for this work. It is possible that it refers to another edition of the *Red Dragon* or *Great Grimoire*.

[401] Amulets and charms that are worn about the body.

Occult Sciences have given rise to the publication of several other works whose worth is more or less justified, but we think that we should refrain from indicating what they are, firstly because their rarity makes them almost impossible to find and then because few people are in a position to verify any practical use from them.

However, (124) we could not resist the pleasure of allowing our readers profiting from a fortuitous hazard,[402] which may allow them to stumble across one of these works, which has helped many of the most fervent adepts of the philosophy of Olivarès[403] to enjoy them with a great amount of happiness.

This most ancient book has for its title COLLECTION OF THE GREATEST SECRETS described by the philosopher Olivarès, familiar in the company of Jesus, at his residence of Goa.

THE END

---

[402] Or *"Lady Luck"*.

[403] Le Comte Duc d'Olivarès. His full title was Don Gaspar de Guzmán y Pimentel Ribera y Velasco de Tovar, or The Count-Duke of Olivares and Duke of San Lúcar la Mayor (1587 1645). He was the Spanish Prime Minister from 1621-1643 and was considered a favourite of King Philip IV of Spain. His attempt to recapture Holland for the Spanish Throne precipitated his involvement in the Thirty Years War (1618–1648) (primarily a religious conflict between Catholics and Protestants).

<u>ADDITONAL TEXTS OF THE "COLLECTION OF SECRETS"</u>

The following text includes additional *'Secrets'* found in the 1670 and/or 1800 (Rome) editions, which are not found in the 1760 edition. It should also be noted that some of the instructions relating to time of day, as well as some references to the various plants and herbs used in folkloric herbal medicine are absent in some of the later texts. This is also true for some of the descriptions of the *'Secrets'*. I have tried to point out these differences as much as possible in the notes, There is also some stylistic variation in the text, especially relating to the usage of *'tu'* and *'vous'*, the two French words for *'you'* in English, although *'tu'* relates to the archaic *'thou'*. Many of the additional secrets are accredited to an occultist called Guidon.

The additional material is interspersed in the common text and where the text ordering is identical, I have referred you to where you can find the corresponding text in the main *Collection of Secrets*. It should be noted that the paging between the different versions is very different.

1800 (ROME) EDITION

(48) **To make three ladies or three gentlemen come to your room after supper.**

Preparation

You should go for three days without extracting any mercury[404] and you will retire upstairs. On the fourth day, as so

on as you have dressed, you will clean and prepare your room from the morning [onwards], doing everything whilst fasting. And you will make it so that no one will spoil the room for the rest of the day and you will make sure that nothing is hanging or hung up around the bed, such as tapestries, cloths, hats, bird cages, curtains etc. and above all, place white sheets on your bed. (49)

Ceremony

At the end of supper, retire secretly to your room, prepared as above. Make a roaring fire; place a white cloth on the table and three chairs around it, and in front of each seat, three loaves of bread made out of wheat and three glasses full of clear, fresh water. Then place a chair or an armchair next to your bed, then go to bed and say the following words:

Conjuration

"*Besticirum consolation veni ad me vertu Creon, Creon, Creon, cantor laudem omnipotentis et non commentur. Star superior carta bient laudem omviestra principiem da montem et inimicos meos ô prostantis vobis et mihi dantes quo passium fieri sui cisibilis.*"[405]

---

[404] *Mercury* was extracted from *cinnabar* and commonly used to treat syphilis, which was fairly prevalent in French society in the 1700's.

[405] Latin: *"Besticirum, consolation, come to me! Virtue of Creon, Creon, Creon. I sing the praises of the Almighty. I do not lie. I am master of the parchment. By thy praise, prince of the Mountain, silence mine enemies and give me the enjoyment of that which you well know."* EL: Corrections to conjuration: Besticirum -> bestiarum (animal); cantor -> canto (sing); commentur -> confundor (mixed together); star -> stat (stand still); carta -> casta (pure); bient -> fiant. EL also gives this amendment to the second line: *'Omnia*

When the three persons have come, they will sit near the fire, drinking, eating, and then they will thank the person, man or woman, who has received them: for (50) if it is a lady who did this ceremony, there will come three gentlemen; and if it is a man, there will come three ladies. These three persons will draw lots between them to determine which one of them will stay with you. That person will sit down in the armchair or the chair that you will have intended for them near your bed and they[406] will stay and chat with you until midnight. And at that hour, that person will go with the other companions, without the need for sending that person away. As far as the two others are concerned, they will stand by the fire while the other will engage you in conversation and while that person is with you, you may interrogate them about any art or any science or anything that you wish and that person will give a positive response on the spot. You may also ask them, if they know of any hidden treasure and they will inform you of the place, the location and the convenient time to retrieve it, even if it is amongst their companions, in order to defend yourself against infernal Spirits, who (51) may be in possession of it and in taking their leave of you, they will give you a ring, which will give you luck in games when it is worn on your finger. And if you place it on the finger of a woman or girl, you will enjoy the use of her on the spot.

Note, that you must leave the window open, so that she can enter. You may repeat this same ceremony as often as you wish.

To make a girl come find you, no matter how wise she may be: operation from a wondrous power from Superior Intelligences.

A star between eleven o'clock and midnight should be noted at the waxing or the waning of the Moon. But before commencing, do the following:

Take some virgin parchment, write the name of the person, whom you wish to make come. The parchment should be cut in the way represented (52) in the first line of the present figure.

---

vestra, principium da mentem et passim mostrare fiam inviu."
[406] This is singular. In French, the word for a *"person"* is feminine, regardless of gender or sex. This language cannot be mirrored in English, as there is no grammatical gender and therefore I use the *"they/them"* convention to denote a single person of either sex.

407

---

[407] The Latin in the image reads — *Consummatom est:* "It is completed"; *Deus est ignis consumens:* "God is a consuming fire".

At the two "NN" mark the place for the names. On the other side, write these words, "*Machidael Barefchas*".[408] Then you will place your parchment on the ground, the names of the person against the earth, with the right foot on it and the left knee on the ground. While looking at the brightest star, you should have a candle of white wax in your right hand, that can burn for an hour, say the following salutation:

Conjuration

"*I salute and conjure you, Oh beautiful Moon and beautiful Star, brilliant light that I hold in my hand, by the air that I breathe, by the air that is in me and by the earth that I touch. I conjure you, by all the names of the Princely Spirits, who preside in you, by the ineffable name On, who created everything, by thee, beautiful Angel Gabriel with the Prince Mercury, Michael and Melchidael. I conjure you (53) anew by all the divine names of God, that you may send to haunt, torment, work on the body, the spirit, the soul and the five senses of nature of N, whose name is written here below. In such manner that she may come to me and accomplish my will and may she have the friendship of no-one in the world, especially for N, while she will have indifference for me. May she not endure, may she be haunted, suffer and be tormented. Come swiftly, therefore, Melchidael, Bareschas, Zazel, Tiriel, Malcha[409] and all those who are under you, I conjure you by the Great Living God, to send her swiftly to accomplish my will. I, N, promise to satisfy you.*"

After having pronounced this conjuration three times, place the candle on the parchment and let it burn. On the following day, take the said parchment and place it in your left shoe and leave it there until the person on whom (54) you have worked has come to find you. The day that you wish her to come should be specified in the conjuration and she will not fail you.

---

[408] The subsequent variations of these names in the text suggest they may be corrupted. See the next note.

[409] This sequence of names is planetary and zodiacal. Malchidiel may be a corruption of Melchidael, the Zodiacal Angel of Aries; Bareschas may be a corruption of Barzabel, the Planetary Spirit of Mars; Zazel is the Planetary Spirit of Saturn; Tiriel is the Planetary Intelligence of Mercury; Malcha is the short form of the Planetary Intelligence of Intelligences for the Moon, Malcha betharsism hed beruah schehalim. These names are found in Agrippa's *De Occulta Philosophia* (1510) published in 1533.

To win at games

This is found on page 48 of the Rome 1760 Edition.

To extinguish a chimney fire

This is found on page 48 of the Rome 1760 Edition. The figure is in the text itself, rather than a referral to an appendix of characters. (55)

To make oneself invisible[410]

This operation is begun on a Wednesday before sunrise, being equipped with seven black beans. Then you take the head of a dead man and one of the beans is placed into the mouth, two others into the nostrils, two others in the eyes and two in the ears. The present character on line 1[411] is then made on this head, then the head is buried with the face towards the heavens. Water it for nine days with excellent brandy water in the mornings before the sun rises. On the eighth day, you will find there the adjourned Spirit,[412] who will ask you, *"What dost thou there?"* You will reply to him, *"I am watering my plant."* He will say to you, *"Give me this bottle and I will water it myself."* You will reply that you do not wish for that. He will ask you to do it one more time. You will refuse him it, until holding his hand, you will see on him the figure similar to the one that you (56) made on the head [of the dead man], which will be hanging from the end of his fingers. In this case, you should be assured, that it is the true Spirit of the head. For something else might surprise you, which would be bad for you and your operation would become fruitless. When you have given him your phial, he will water it himself and you will take your leave. On the next day, which is the ninth day, you will return to that place. There you will find your mature beans. You will take them and you will place one of them into your mouth, then you will look at yourself in a mirror; if you do not see yourself, then all is well. You will do the same with all the others, testing them in the mouth of a child and all those that do not have any worth,[413] must be buried back where the head is.

---

[410] Compare the *'secret'* found in *A Collection of Magical Secrets*, 2008:59.

[411] The characters are given on page 21 of the 1670 Edition.

[412] That is to say, the Spirit of the dead man.

[413] That is to say, ineffectual.

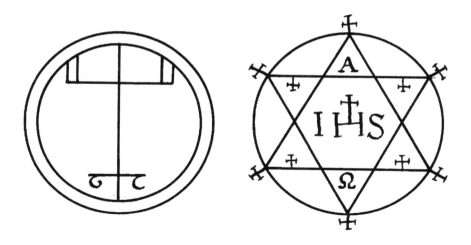

To have gold or silver or a hand of glory (57 – 59)

This is found on pages 48/49 of the Rome 1760 Edition.

Garter[414] (59 – 61)

This is found on pages 51/52 of the Rome 1760 Edition.

To be impervious against all manner of weapons (61 – 62)

This is found on page 53 of the Rome 1760 Edition.

---

[414] There is no mention of what the garter is intended for in this text.

415

To make a person come [to you] (63)

"*Bundle of Firewood, burn the heart, the body, the soul, the blood, the spirit, the comprehension of N., by the fire, by the heavens, by the earth, by the rainbow, by Mars, Mercury, Venus, Jupiter, Feppé,*[416] *Feppé, Feppé, Elera and in the name of all the devils, bundle of firewood, burn the heart, the body, the soul, the blood the spirit, the comprehension of N. until he comes to accomplish all my desires and wishes. Come in lightning, in embers and in tempest; Santos Quisor, Carracos, Arné, Tourne, may he not*

---

[415] The French words around the edge say "*Obeissez a vos superieurs et leur soyez soumis parce qu'ils y prennent garde*", which translates as "*Obey your leaders and submit to their authority, for they keep watch over you.*" (*Hebrews 13:17*).

[416] EL: changes this repeated word to Phoebé (brilliant), a title used for the Greek lunar goddess Artemis, and hence referring here to the Moon.

sleep, nor repose in any place, nor do anything, nor eat, not pass a river, nor mount a horse, nor speak to any man, woman or daughter, until he hath come to accomplish all my desires and wishes."

To make a girl dance naked

Write on virgin parchment the first character of the present (64) figure with bats' blood. Then place it on a consecrated stone so that a Mass may be said over it.[417] After this, when you wish to make use of it, place this character under the threshold of the door where the person is to pass. She will barely have crossed over this place, when you will see her enter into a frenzy, undressing herself until she is naked and if the character is not removed,[418] she will dance until she is dead, with grimaces and contortions that cause pity rather than lust.

---

[417] The characters are found on page 24 of the 1670 edition.
[418] Another figure is found on page 35 of the 1670 edition.

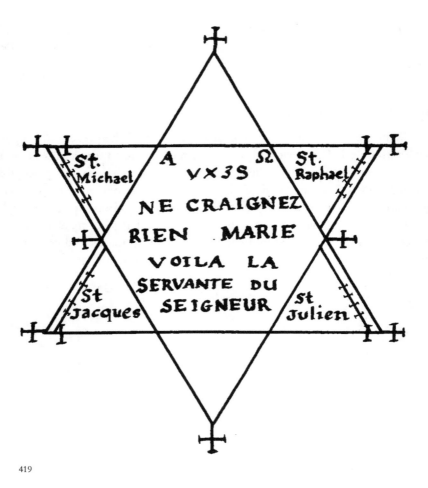

419

---

419 The hexagon in the centre contains the Greek letters Alpha and Omega and the sequence VX3S, followed by the French words *"ne craignez rien Marie voila la servante du seigneur"*, meaning *"Fear nothing, Mary, behold God's handmaiden"*. The outer triangles contain the names of St Raphael, St Julien, St Jacques and St Michael.

420

To see a vision in the night of what you wish to see, in the past or the future (64–65)

This is found on pages 54/55 of the Rome 1760 Edition.

To "nail"[421] (65–66)

This is found on pages 55/56 of the Rome 1760 Edition.

---

[421] The full description in the other edition is *"To use a nail to make someone suffer"*.

To prevent a person from sleeping the whole night, and make him have no rest, until he has spoken to you, even though he wished you a mortal ill and may have been far from you. (67)

The night on which you want to perform this secret, be the last person of the house to retire to bed, when you have got into bed, you will have prepared the fire in the hearth, and particularly, place a lit wood brand against the chimney. Place the palm of your left hand on a place on the chimney that is dark and smoked, holding it closed and open, you will say these words seven times:

"Cinque furono li appicati, linque furono, li tana liati vi scongiro per Béelzébut che linque vi fate ache date à tormentar il cuore et la viscere[422] *(of so and so N.) for my love. Amen.'*[423]

When you have said them seven times, push the wood brand right to the front of the embers and (68) tap the palm of your hand against the black spot of the chimney three times and cover your fire with ash and go to sleep. You will see that the man or woman that you intended to come,[424] will not be able to live nor endure until he has satisfied your desire. This is one of the rare secrets that Necromancy has invented.

To make oneself appear to be accompanied by many (68–69)

This is found on pages 56/57 of the Rome 1760 Edition.

To be wounded by no weapon (69)

This is found on page 57 of the Rome 1760 Edition.

---

[422] Italian: *"Five were the hanged men, five they were. those which are bound with chains, I conjure you by Beelzebut, who are become five and ye torment the heart and bowels (of NN)."*
[423] Interesting that the writer used Italian here, rather than Latin, suggesting that this may have been extra material inserted into the document and also suggesting that the scribe did not know enough Latin to create his own conjurations.
[424] Lit. *"The one whose intention you will have done".*

To enjoy the use of[425] whomever you wish. Secret of Father Girard[426]

Go for three days without any extract of mercury before swallowing a nutmeg.[427] On the fourth day, whilst fasting, you will say to God, *"The torum cultin, cultorum, bultin, bultotum,*[428] *approach me, my companion."* You should swallow the nutmeg, saying, *"Approach, etc."* With that done, when you (70) go to the commode, you will suffer no trouble with the nutmeg. This secret is good for your whole life, without being obliged to repeat it. You only need to say the last three words while blowing through your nose or embracing all those by whom you will wish to be loved.

To make a weapon fail

This is found on page 57 of the Rome 1760 Edition. There are no instructions in this edition, just the invocation.

For Pleurisy

This is found on page 58 of the Rome 1760 Edition. Again, there are no instructions, just the invocation, with the minor variance the name *'Biz'* replaces the name *'Bix'.*[429]

For fevers

This is found on page 58 of the Rome 1760 Edition. There is no mention of how to treat the other types of fever in this edition.

---

[425] Euphemism for seducing and taking advantage of someone sexually.

[426] In the 1670 Edition, this is called *"The Secret love charm of Father Girard".* Father Girard was a Jesuit who was put on trial for using magic to seduce a certain Catherine Cadière.

[427] See the note above for the use of mercury. Nutmeg is thought to be an aphrodisiac in folklore. It is also has hallucinogenic properties, when taken in large quantities.

[428] EL: *"torum cultin, cultorum, bultin, bultotum".*

[429] Both names would be pronounced similarly in French, /biːs/ or /biːz/.

To stop loss of blood

This is found on page 59 of the Rome 1760 Edition. However, in this version, there are no extended instructions and in addition, this edition has an addition at the end:

"...apply it to the forehead, or write: "Consummatum est"".[430] (71)

Against a sword strike

This is found on page 60 of the Rome 1760 Edition. There is no instruction about procuring coloured ribbon in this edition, just the conjuration, which is slightly different: *"Buoni jacum, I have only to make from thee."*

For when you are going into action

This is found on page 60 of the Rome 1760 Edition. (72)

To extinguish fire

This is found on page 61 of the Rome 1760 Edition. However, there is no mention of using wet hay in this edition to extinguish the fire.

For burns

This is found on pages 61/62 of the Rome 1760 Edition. There is no mention of using vinegar compresses in this edition.

For headaches

This is found on page 62 of the Rome 1760 Edition. There is no mention of mixing ground black pepper with *eau-de-vie* in this edition.

For Stomach Flux (72 – 73)

This is found on pages 62/63 of the Rome 1760 Edition. There is no mention of the use of plantain juice in this edition.

---

[430] In the 1670 Edition, it is written: *"You can replace INRI by "Consummatum est"".*

To prevent [someone] from eating at the table

This is found on page 63 of the Rome 1760 Edition. There is no mention of the use of burning Asafœtida in this edition.

To extinguish fire

This is found on page 63 of the Rome 1760 Edition. In this edition, there is no reference made to the similar *'secret'* earlier on in the text, whereas there is in the other edition,

To prevent copulation (73 – 74)

This is found on pages 63/64 of the Rome 1760 Edition. There is no mention of when to perform this operation, or what characters to use, as there are in the other edition.

For Games

This is found on page 64 of the Rome 1760 Edition. There is no indication of the weather conditions on this edition. Nor are there instructions on how to carry the scapular made of clover leaves.

To stop a serpent

This is found on pages 64/65 of the Rome 1760 Edition. There is no mention of the paper having to be dipped in an alum solution beforehand, nor mention of the words having to be written in the blood of a kid goat in this edition. (75)

To prevent a dog from biting and barking

While looking at the dog, say three times, *"The barbaric arch, the heart breaks, the tail is hung, the key of St Peter shuts your mouth until tomorrow."*

For ringworm of the hair

This is found on page 65 of the Rome 1760 Edition. There is no mention of how long the rite is to be performed for, nor is there any mention of a poultice being used in this edition.

For games of dice (75 – 76)

This is found on pages 65/66 of the Rome 1760 Edition. No reference is made to the scapular mentioned in the other edition.

To remove a fish-bone from the throat

This is found on page 66 of the Rome 1760 Edition. There is no mention of using a leek for the operation in this edition.

To not tire of walking

This is found on pages 66/67 of the Rome 1760 Edition. No mention is made of the three silk ribbons and how to use them in this edition.

To win at all games

This is found on page 66 of the Rome 1760 Edition. There is no further commentary in this edition, as there is in the other one.

To avoid undergoing interrogation

Swallow a slip of paper, on which the following has been written with your own blood: *"Aglas, Aglanos, Algadenas, Imperiequeritis, tria pendent corpora ramis dis meus et gestas in medio et divina potestas dimeas clamator,*[431] *sed jestas ad astra (77) levatur"*.[432] Or even, *"Tel, Bel, Quel, Caro, Man, Aqua."*

---

[431] EL: Imperiequeritis -> imparibus meritis (change made in black ink; those below in red); dis meus -> Dismas; medio et divina -> medio est divina; clamator -> damnatur.

[432] This is a corruption of a medieval verse based on *Luke 23:39-43* regarding the crucifixion: *"Imparibus meritis, tria pendet corpora ramis, Dismas et Gesmas in media est divina potestas; Gesmas damnatur, Dismas levatur ad astra."* This translates: *"Not equal in their merits hang three bodies hanging from the wood (i.e. crucified) Dismas and Gesmas, and amidst the power of God. Gesmas is doomed, and Dismas is lifted to the stars."* Lea (1957) records this charm as being used by witches undergoing torture. It is also found in *The Magical Works of Henri Cornelius Agrippa*, 1744:99.

Secrets and Counter-Charms by Guidon,[433] practitioner in healing through occult ways.[434]

The secrets that are going to follow as sure as guaranteed: Guidon, who practices them all the time, has made, through their use, cures, which prove that one can no longer be in a state of doubt about them. All the lands of Caux[435] and Normandy are convinced of them. He performs his operations in public, as well as in private; guided by a charitable zeal, he undertakes for the destitute, as also for the opulent with the same spirit. In this way, he has acquired the esteem and the protection of respectable people known to him. He works tirelessly to destroy evil magic and regards the authors of such spells with horror. (78)

Guidon's practice, when it concerns dispossessing[436]

The ancient rituals were a great resource to him. He omitted neither Conjurations, nor Exorcisms, Gospels, nor Prayers. He removes only the places where the dead are mentioned, with Signs of the Cross, and irrational animals. He uses holy water, most often baptismal water, which he sprinkles in the form of a cross over the madman with a consecrated branch from the boxwood tree.[437] He also makes the sign on the forehead of the cursed man with his thumb dipped into the very same water. During the ceremony, his head is bare, as are also the heads of the sick man and the assistants. When he works on dumb animals, in place of holy water, he casts salt over them, prepared in the way that we are going to talk about. He continues his operation with the prayer from the *Enchiridion*, printed in Rome in 1660, on page 43. Then he takes some salt in a bowl, which he exorcises with some of the (79) blood drawn from one of the cursed animals. He stirs everything, saying:

---

[433] Refer to Brian P. Copenhaver's *"Symphorien Champier and the reception of the occultist tradition in renaissance France"* Mouton 1978.

[434] In the 1670 Edition, this is just titled *"Magical Secrets and Counter-Charms"*.

[435] The *"Pays de Caux"* is an area of Normandy in northern France that is known for its chalk plateaus.

[436] In the 1670 Edition, this is entitled, *"Guidon's practice, when it is a matter of destroying a curse placed on a human being or an animal."*

[437] The *Boxwood* was dedicated to Hades, as it was a symbol of immortality on account of it being an evergreen tree. It was used medicinally for the treatment of wounds and intoxicants, however it is also highly toxic and can cause death.

"Beati tornitis omnes Joannes Baptizantes et agentes."[438]

Afterwards, he performs a *Novena* at home, which is to be recited for nine days whilst fasting, and the Prayer from the *Enchiridion*, which will be indicated.

To break and destroy all evil spells[439]

This is found on page 67 of the Rome 1760 Edition. Presumably this and the next item are from the Practice of Guidon. (80)

The Great Exorcism to dispossess either the human creature or irrational animals (80–84)

This is found on pages 68 - 72 of the Rome 1760 Edition. It can be assumed that this is the prayer mentioned from the *Enchiridion*, as practised by Guidon. (85)

To remove all spells and to summon the person who caused the evil deed (85–87)

This is found on pages 72-75 of the Rome 1760 Edition.

The Castle of the Fair-Protector[440] for horses (87–93)

This is found on pages 75 - 81 of the Rome 1760 Edition. However, in this edition, there is an extra line that does not appear in the other edition, which appears at the end:

"We intend to reprint the Enchiridion of Pope Leo on the same subject, in which is attached the discoveries and the experiences that Guidon practised surprisingly successfully." This confirms that all these *'secrets'* are from Guidon.

---

[438] Corrupted Latin: *"John the Baptist grant us powerful blessings."*
[439] In the 1670 Edition, this is entitled *"Another, to destroy all curses affecting animals"*
[440] Note how the language is slightly different in this edition, here it is the *"Castle of the Fair Protector, for horses"* as opposed to the *"Castle of the Fair One, a Guard for horses"*. The variance may be due to a copy error.

Guard for whatever you will (93–94)

This is found on page 81 of the Rome 1760 Edition.

Another Guard (94–95)

This is found on pages 81/82 of the Rome 1760 Edition.

Guard against mange, scabies and sheep-pox (95–97)

This is found on pages 82-84 of the Rome 1760 Edition.

Guard against mange (97–98)

This is found on page 85 of the Rome 1760 Edition.

Guard for preventing wolves from entering into a field where the Sheep are (98–100)

This is found on pages 85/86 of the Rome 1760 Edition.

The Marionettes of Protection

This is found on page 87 of the Rome 1760 Edition. The mention that *"only the pure of heart will succeed in this operation"* is omitted in this edition.

Guard for horses (100–101)

This is found on pages 87/88 of the Rome 1760 Edition.

Guard for the flock (101–103)

This is found on pages 88-90 of the Rome 1760 Edition.

Another Guard for sheep (103–106)

This is found on pages 90/91 of the Rome 1760 Edition.

Guard against rabbits (106–109)

This is found on pages 93/94 of the Rome 1760 Edition. The last sentence is significantly different in this edition:

"We are intending to give protections of another sort in the French translation of Agrippa and in the Clavicules[441] of Solomon. To these works, we will add the secrets in our experience."

To control[442]

Two remnants of hay are taken. One must have a knot in the middle, the other is placed in a cross over the knot, then you pronounce above it:

"Anchor of God, anchor of the Virgin, anchor of the Devil; Satan, hie thee to all the devils."

The cross is thrown at the nose of the animal, pronouncing the same words and with one knee on the ground. By this method, you may carry the animal on your shoulders or elsewhere, no matter how vicious it may be, without risk of being bitten by it. (110)

To be imperviable[443]

"Valanda jacem rafit massif excorbis anter volganda zazar,[444] brother, lend me thy hand; Bourbelet, barlet, Amer, gather around me, as Judas betrayed our Lord."

The slip is carried around the neck and when in danger, pronounce the same words. It is through this method, that Guidon, attacked by two cavalrymen at an inn in Fauville,[445] was saved from well over five hundred sword hits. After this assault, he returned to his home calmly.

---

[441] Or *"Keys"*.

[442] Or *"bridle"* an animal. In the 1670 Edition, this is entitled, *"To soothe (or calm) an animal"*.

[443] In the 1670 Edition, this is entitled, *"To escape all attack, no matter how violent it may be"*. You are advised in writing, *"you write on a slip of paper"*.

[444] Nonsensical or corrupt Latin, with an element of Occitan.

[445] Situated in the *Pays de Caux*, 29 miles (46.4 kms) north of the port of *Le Havre*.

To discover Treasures

While being at a place where you suspect treasure may be hidden, while striking against the ground with your left heel three times, and making a turn to the left, say:

"Sadies satani agir fons toribus:[446] *come to me, Seradon, who shall be called Sarietur."*

Start over three times in a row. If there is any treasure in the place, (111) you will know it, because something will be revealed to you in your ear.

To stop horses and carriages and to lead a person astray (111–112)

This is found on pages 96/97 of the Rome 1760 Edition. Note that in that edition, only *'Horses and Carriages'* are mentioned and nothing is said about *'leading a person astray'*. In this edition, however, no instructions are given for what to write on the paper and how the paper should be.

Counter-Charm

This is found on page 98 of the Rome 1760 Edition.

For the lambs to become[447] beautiful and very strong

This is found on page 98 of the Rome 1760 Edition.

Against firearms (112–113)

This is found on pages 98/99 of the Rome 1760 Edition. See note 172

---

[446] Very corrupted Latin, referring to something about Satan, land and source, so possibly originally asking Satan to reveal the source of treasure in the land?
[447] In the other edition, this is given as *"reviennent"* - *"come back, return"*.

For ulcerous lesions;[448] fevers[449]

This is found on page 99 of the Rome 1760 Edition. There is an additional sentence in this edition, which relates to fevers, which is appended to the text and reads as thus:

"These same words, written on paper and carried hung around the neck for nine days, heal fevers."

For glanders and abdominal cramps in horses (113–114)

This is found on pages 99/100 of the Rome 1760 Edition. There is no mention of the herbal remedies that can be applied in this edition.

To heal sprains and twists

This is found on pages 100/101 of the Rome 1760 Edition. There is no mention of the compresses that can be used in this edition.

To prevent a flock from touching the grain, passing between two furrows (114–115)

This is found on page 101 of the Rome 1760 Edition.

To make the hæmorrhage pass

This is found on page 102 of the Rome 1760 Edition. Slight variant in the Spelling of *'Sathan'* (which is what is found here).

For growths or asthma

Open the mouth of the Horse, blow three times into it pronouncing the words below.

("In tes dalame bouis, vins Divernas Sathan.")

---

[448] Literally, *"clumps".*
[449] *"Fevers"* is not mentioned in the Rome 1760 edition.

For mumps

This is found on page 102 of the Rome 1760 Edition. (116)

For scabies and ringworm in animals

This is found on page 102 of the Rome 1760 Edition. Clearly there have been some copying errors creeping in (or maybe even corrections) as the earlier text is slightly different: *'Gupin'* is written as *'Lupin'* and there are some spelling errors in the text. It reads, *"Lupin while shoeing has almost the big one, for he hath made me do it."* It is even different from the similar invocation in the text (see Protection for whatever you will). Even so, the invocation is very garbled, even in the French, and the translation is an intelligent guess as to its meaning.

For hæmorrhoids

This is found on pages 102/103 of the Rome 1760 Edition. The remedy using elder mixed into butter to rub onto the hæmorrhoids is not mentioned in this edition. (117)

For epilepsy or falling sickness[450]

This is found on page 103 of the Rome 1760 Edition.

Enchantment for stopping Blood

"Sanguis manè in te sicut fecit Christus in sanguis manè in tua vena sicut Christus in sua pœnat sanguis manè fixus sicut quando fuit crucifixus.'[451]

Repeat three times.

---

[450] This *'secret'* and the next one are also found in the 1670 Edition.
[451] This charm is previously found as *'For a bloody flux, or rather an issue of blood'*, Book XII, ch.18 of *Discoverie of Witchcraft*, Scot, 1584. The English Member of Parliament and diarist Samuel Pepys (1633-1703) recorded this charm in his diary 31st December 1664-1st January 1665 without any comment. The popularity of this charm may be seen in the fact that it is also found in the 17th century Icelandic Grimoire, the *Galdabrok*. Latin: *"Good Blood, in thee as did Christ, in the good blood in thy vein as Christ in his atonement, good blood held as when he was crucified"*.

Counter-charm

'Ecce Crucem Domini, fugite partes adversæ, vicit leo de tribu Judah, radix David.'[452]

Against Fire

'In te, Domine, speravi, non confundar in æternum.'[453] (118)

For fevers[454]

'God hath come into the World to redeem us of our sins. He fasted when he was thirty three years and three days old. He was sold to the Jews for thirty deniers.[455] *May Tertiary Fever, Quartan Fever, of whatever quality that it be, not endure in my body. In the name of Jesus, who was fixed to the tree of the Cross, where he spilled his blood for our sins. Saint Mary, pray for me: Saint Michael, preserve me: Jesus, Mary, Saint Joseph, aid me; Mary Saint Catherine, preserve me.'* Here, the name of the febricitant[456] must be placed, who must carry the above around his neck, saying five Paters and five Aves every day whilst fasting, before an image of the Virgin.

END[457]

---

[452] This dates to the 13th century CE and is known as the Brief/Letter of St Anthony (of Padua). It was usually written in the shape of a cross and reads: *"Behold the Cross of the Lord! Flee ye adversaries! The Lion of the Tribe of Judah, The Root of David has conquered [Hallelujah]."*

[453] Latin: *"In thee, O Lord, have I hoped, let me never be confounded".* (*Psalm 30:2*) Also found in the *Enchiridion of Pope Leo III* and *Les Oeuvres Magiques* d'Henri Corneille Agrippa, 1744:90. This is an abbreviated form of the charm found in *The Keys of Rabbi Solomon* (Wellcome 4669), which goes: Write this verse on the chimney with fired charcoal, *"In te, Domine, speravi non confunduar in æternaum, in justitia tua libera mē"*; and at the end, *"Tetragrammaton consummatum est."*

[454] See note about fevers above on page 70 (also see p.59 of the Rome 1760 edition). In the 1670 Edition, this is called, *"Cure for Fevers".*

[455] A French coin, that comes from the Roman coin *"denarius".*

[456] *"person with the fever".*

[457] EL: ends his copy with a note of the publisher - Pommeret and Guénot, 2 rue Mignon.

APPENDICES

THE GERMAN EDITION OF THE GRIMOIRE OF POPE HONORIUS[458]

The So-Called Grimoire or The Great Grimoire of Pope Honorius[459]

AD + 1220

THE BEGINNING OF THIS BOOK RUNS THUS:

The Master of this Book, before he begins, should prepare for the Great Work through Confession, Communion and a Fast of three days, taking unto himself no other nourishment other than water and bread, with a humble heart and with his sins arraigned through the direct effects of Almighty God and not through his own will. He should don a surplice and a stole and have consecrated wax candles in readiness, and should go from one corner [of the room] to the other, first towards the East, then bowing towards the other corners opposing the heavens and say as follows:

"Ariel, southerly[460] Spirit of God, whether thou beest now in the East, West or North,[461] thou who openest treasures and concealest them, I conjure thee by the Almighty, who created Heaven and Earth from nothing, by the Judge of the Quick and the Dead! I conjure thee by God the Father + God the Son + and God the Holy Ghost + and by all the other names of the Great God, Elion + Tetragrammaton +, I conjure thee by the

---

[458] The existing translation in the Trident edition of their *Grimoire of Pope Honorius* was found to have numerous errors in it and certain difficult passages had been left untranslated. It was therefore deemed appropriate to make a completely new translation of this work and include it as part of our appendices.

[459] Note by the transcriber Scheibler: *"I give this from a manuscript in the infernal library of a Swabian farmer, whose nonsense he copied from somewhere for the purpose of exorcising dæmons, though countless spelling mistakes make it completely ridiculous. Those [mistakes] that were unable to be unravelled have been printed word for word from this manuscript."*

[460] The German is *Mittag* and like the French *Midi*, refers to the South, rather than the Midday Sun.

[461] Like *Mittag*, other points of the compass are referred to as directions of the *"Rising [Sun], [Sun]set and Midnight"*.

Holy Virgin Mary, I conjure thee by all the Angels and Archangels, Seraphim and Cherubim, Thrones and Dominions, Prophets and Evangelists, Apostles and all the Holy Martyrs, Confessors + and all the Holy Virgins, by the Old and the New Testaments +, by the holy Sacraments of the Altar +, by the Sun, Moon and all the Planets, and by he, who hath cast thee into Hell +, by he, who hath given himself up to suffer pain and death upon the beam of the Cross, to appear unto me here in a human form, without causing fright nor fear, neither harming my soul nor body, neither myself nor those, who are with me. I command thee to answer every question in accordance with the truth. Firstly, I command thee by all the highest aforementioned names to deliver unto me treasures of gold, silver and costly pearls that thou hast under thy power, so that everything that I and those with me have need thereof, is delivered unto myself as also to those that are in my company, without gaining power over us, neither in life nor after death. I command thee, abandon these treasures and depart hence in peace +."

If the Conjurer is fearless and courageous, then no suffering can befall him. Behold the Conjuration of Pope Honorius the Great.

"I further conjure thee and command all you[462] *Hosts of Spirits to appear to me as soon as I call upon you with these names that are contained in this Book and moreover ye are to appear unto me in a human and pleasant form, as ye are commanded, and this without causing harm to us, neither in body nor soul, neither with an uproar or with fire, so that ye may forthwith retreat from here after the conjuration, without any tarry or delay, as is written herein, and do that, which I command, quickly and completely and totally, after ye have received your power, and this without lies nor falsehood. And should one of the Spirits, whose names are recorded in this book live in another place and cannot appear, let him send me another Spirit of a similar power as the other, so that he may carry out the same task and let him bind himself with an oath to obey my commandment, or the commandment of the person in possession of this Book. I shall compel you to wade in brimstone and fire for four thousand years, if ye do not follow and perform any single commandment. Ye will also call those, who possess the office and power to accept this Book, to which your devil must appear instantly, and what has been commanded of you, to bring it into effect, for I doubt it not, that ye will fail to appear, when the reward for your labours is denied you."*

---

[462] The German text shifts between *"du"*, you singular and *"Sie/Ihr"*, you plural quite liberally. I have followed the text as faithfully as possible, although, of course, in English, it could just be rendered as *"you"* throughout, but then you would lose the feeling of the invocations a little.

Note: This Book should be consecrated and a Mass to the Holy Trinity should be read before it is opened. The Formulæ for the Conjurations should be spoken immediately after the Transubstantiation of the Bread and the Wine.

"I conjure thee, Book, to be useful to all, who desire thy services in all of their affairs. I also conjure thee through the Power of the Blood of Jesus Christ, which is in this Chalice, to prove[463] *thy usefulness to all those, who shall read thee."*

Note: After this, the Book is consecrated in the Name of the Most Holy Trinity three times over, thereby completing the [Consecration] when the sign of the Cross is made.

"I employ thee in order to constrain and compel the wicked Spirits in the Name of the Father +, of the Son +, and the of Holy Ghost +, so that they may have no power to step into the Circle and harm anyone."

THIS IS THE CIRCLE.

"Let all Spirits obey us through the Power of the Almighty God."

AFTER THIS:

"Forsake me not, Oh Lord, my God! Turn not away from me, come to my succour, God of my Salvation! Almighty God, I pray thee to consecrate and bless this Book through the Most Holy Names that are written within, so that it may be completely effectual and that the Spirits from all places may come, wherever they may be, to obey thee and do everything that is contained in this Book according to my will, as often and as many times as I command, without harm to either my body nor soul, through the Power of Our Lord Jesus Christ, to whom Honour and Glory is due, forever and ever, Amen!"

---

[463]Is it possible that the verb was conjugated incorrectly and that the verb should be *"bewahren"*, *"to preserve"* rather than *"bewähren"*, *"to prove"*, which is mostly used intransitively or reflectively.

OPEN CONFESSION OF SINS

"Lord Jesus Christ, through thy ineffable mercy, forgive me and take pity upon me when I call upon thee, in the Holy Names of the Father + of the Son + and of the Holy Ghost +. Let my word and prayer be pleasing unto thee, through the invocation of all the Holy Names, which are consecrated in this Book through the Holy Names of Jesus Christ, Alpha and Omega, Elison Anathema Adonai Emmanuel Sabaoth; through all the Names, which are permitted to be pronounced, and through all the Holy Names, which are written in this Book, through their Sanctity and Power, let this [Book] also be blessed, through the Divine Might and the Holy Sacraments of the most precious Body and Blood, so that it may receive all power and efficacy, that all Operations with the Spirits [are performed] through the assistance of our Lord Jesus Christ, to whom is due Honour and Glory, forever and ever, Amen."

THE OPEN CONFESSION OF SIN

"Invincible, Invariable, Immortal, Merciful, Glorious, Immortal God! Be not mindful of my sins, but grant the prayer of the Sinner, and even though I am unworthy of thy grace, nevertheless bless my undertakings, so that I may receive the power to subdue and compel the Spirits of Hell, so that they may obey my call and present themselves; and when I permit them to depart, may they yield through thy Holy Names Ena, Elion, Gen + Aglat, Golat +, which, when they are pronounced, stop the sea in its course and make the Earth tremble, extinguish the fire, disperse all the waters, [and make] the Spirits of Hell flee before thy Mighty Name."

"En, Alpha + et Omega et Ela + Elaya + Adonai + Ange + Avenaege +, may this Book be consecrated and may all the Spirits, whose Names are recorded within obey me. Beyzacdain, who ruleth over all, to whom Honour and Glory are due, Forever and ever, Amen!"

Now quickly don the stole and surplice, take a lighted, consecrated candle in hand, asperse with Holy Water mixed with centaury[464] and then wrap this Book up in clean, consecrated linen, as the innocent child, Jesus must have been swaddled. Then, for three consecutive Fridays, lay it under the Altar Cloth, beside the Gospel of St John, under the Holy Mass, and after that bind it together crosswise with a linen cloth and keep it safe in a clean place until you have need thereof.

---

[464] A herb of the gentian family that produces pink flowers and is used in herbal medicine for dyspepsia and other gastric problems.

CONJURATION OF THE SPIRITS OF THE AIR PRAYER

"Adonai! My heavenly and kindly Father, take pity upon me, wretched sinner that I am and extend thine Almighty arm this day, Amen! Strengthen me against the Spirits, finally grant me, in consideration of the godly perfection, to praise and extol thy Holy Name, Jesus Christ. I pray to thee, Oh God, My Lord, I call from the innermost part of my heart, so that the Spirits, whom I shall summon will have to come and bring that, which I require and answer all questions without deceit nor ambiguity, neither causing harm to myself nor to anyone, who is near me, either in soul or in body, neither frighten us through uproar and may they obey all my commandments through thee, my Creator, thou, who livest and reignest forever and ever, Amen!"

NAMES OF THE SPIRITS OF THE AIR

Note: This prayer is spoken one day before the Spirits of the Air are to be summoned, also a Mass to the Holy Ghost should be read. On the following day, you should retire to a solitary place and speak the following Prayer, whereafter appeal to the named Angels, call them to assist you and say:

"I pray to you, ye Spirits, that ye may be favourable unto me in that, which I desire, in accordance with what I require, that ye may come to me forthwith, to help and assist me in all things that I shall hereafter request, and that ye may bring [all things] to a good and happy outcome. As many of you as there may be, I conjure you through Agios Otheos + Isvios + Atthonalos + Alpha + et Omega + and through the power and merit of the glorious Virgin Mary, the mother of Jesus Christ, and through the power of the Holy Names of the Great and Living God do I conjure you to bring my will to completion forthwith. Chanca Teristrison + Tan Ha Teritrisa Tabue Tabrena Alitia Alpha et Omega Adonai Jehova Adonai Adonai At Honabos Agios Ishiros Adonai Tetragrammaton Adonai. I conjure thee[465] stubborn Spirit to appear to me without delay, without uproar and in a pleasant form, through the almighty power of the Holy and Powerful Names of the Great and Living God Adonai + Sadai + Aa + Agios + Emanuel + Agios + Atheos + Jesiros + Athanatos + Alpha + et Omega Holy Lord God Zabaoth +. This word bindeth the Holy Ghost, Most Holy Trinity, Creator of all beings; I conjure thee anew, thou aforementioned Spirit to appear to me in a graceful form in the Name of God + Adonai + El + Elion + Elia + Adonai + Sadai + Lux +

---

[465] The German reverts to *"du/dich"* here, rather than *"ihr/euch"* - *"thou/thee"*, *"ye/you"*.

Tetragrammaton ✠ Alpha ✠ et Omega ✠ Messias ✠ Soter ✠ Emanuel ✠ Sabaoth ✠ Sapiens ✠ Victor ✠ Via ✠ Veritas ✠ Vita ✠ Agios ✠ Otheos and through all the other Names of God, which are known to Mortals and Immortals, I compel you, to appear here now. I conjure thee anew through all the Glory and Might of the divine Majesty, through the 24 Elect, who stand before the face of God and daily and unceasingly call to him, "Holy, Holy, Holy is the Lord Zabaoth ✠" and in the Power of God the Father ✠ and of the Son ✠ and of the Holy Ghost ✠ by the authority of our Lord Jesus Christ of Nazareth, the Crucified. I conjure thee anew to forthwith yield to my control, without violence, with diligence and in a graceful form, and perform all my commandments in the Name of the Father ✠ of the Son ✠ and of the Holy Ghost ✠ Amen!"

END OF THE FIRST CONJURATION

THE NAMES OF THE SPIRITS OF THE AIR:

Michael, Gabriel, Gamael, Raphael, Serachiel, Anael, Kaphpiel.

THE METHOD FOR DISCHARGING THE SPIRITS

"I conjure thee, Spirit N.N., who hath appeared to me, to yield before me in peace and go to the place that God hath intended for thee for Eternity, through Our Lord Jesus Christ, who liveth and reigneth forever and ever. I command thee to appear, as oft as I shall call upon thy names and stamp thrice upon the earth with thy foot, may thou accomplish my desires in the place, whence I shall summon thee."

Note: Each Spirit should be called by his name and then they will fulfil all wishes. They are called: **Lucifer, Beelzebub, Astharoth, Asmodai, Leviathan, Barbuit, Berbigot, Genap, Dariston, Aeol**. Whoever has complete knowledge of these Spirits, will not then find it difficult to learn what is occurring in all 4 quarters of the World, and he can make the Spirits fulfil all [his] desires obediently. They have to serve you, whether you are presently at home or beneath an open sky. There are 24 of these Spirit Princes in number, who partly rule in the Water and partly rule upon the Earth. They are summoned at the same time. Each one has his particular office. The first three give their Sigil and Seal, as is desired of them. In them, you may behold whatever you wished. They may be summoned at any time, but only during the waning Moon. The three others have the power to make you invisible and carry your belongings from one place to another, especially through the means of a stone, which they will give to you by the start of the third day of the waning Moon, as soon as you compel them to do so. Three others of the named Spirits bring what you desire from distant places, whether it be gold or silver, but only on the fifth day of the waning Moon, when it is setting. The last ones arrange gatherings and you call them on the eleventh day at the setting of the waning Moon.

LUCIUS CASER[466]

The first three Prince Spirits are called: **Molo**, **Nape**, **Ido**, the next three: **Tonsin**, **Agathoe**, **Amiaden**, the three that are the last but one: **Altaino**, **Jusatine**, **Driades**, the three last ones: **Migola**, **Tausata**, **Xotuda**. You should note that **Lucius** is the same name as **Lucifer**. He sometimes goes forth from his place and compels them to follow the bidding of those orders of Spirits who rank beneath him, those in turn to [follow the bidding] of those superior to them. They must be summoned according to rank and office by the conjurer with a strong voice.

THE CONJURATION OF ASTHAROTH

*"In the Name of the Father ✠ and of the Son ✠ and of the Holy Ghost, Amen! May the Divinity bless me and preserve me ✠. May the immense Loving-Kindness protect me ✠ I am shielded by the Glory ✠ and the Unity ✠ the Might of the Father ✠ the Wisdom of the Son ✠ I am enlightened by the Power of the Holy Ghost ✠ **Alpha** and **Omega** God and Man through this holy invocation may I alone be shielded and protected bountifully in the Name of the Father ✠ in the Name of the Son ✠ and of the Holy Ghost ✠ Amen!"*

*"I pray to thee, Mighty Lord, Jesus Christ that thou mayest permit me to conjure **Astaroth** by the Day of dreadful Judgement and by the ascent of the Lord into Heaven and his descent into Hell, by the deprivation, captivity and death of our Lord Jesus Christ, by his resurrection, by the Almighty God of Creation, the visible and invisible, by everything that is in Him, towards the East, South, West or North, upon the Land or in the Sea, in the light of the Sun or under the Earth, that he may appear to me forthwith*

---

[466] E. M. Butler (1949) notes this in his discussion of the German text by Scheible as another name for Lucifer

and without delay before me, in human form and without any uproar, and answer my questions truthfully and without guile, and be submissive and obedient unto me, as our Lord Jesus Christ was submissive unto his Father at his death."

Note: **Astaroth** comes in the form of a young woman, gives gold, silver, houses etc. You should call her nine times. She gives hidden profits and she is invoked for these attributes.

Naema appears as crowned woman on a tall horse, teaches secret knowledge and heals sickness; her Kingdom is in the West. **Agarus**, an old man, teaches languages and gives Power and Might. **St. Petrus**[467] willingly gives information, he shows treasures, brings silver, gold and whatever else is demanded. **Soas**, a crowned Prince, reveals treasures, gives true answers. **Gamoet**, a King, reveals treasures. **Ampheron**, an old man, reveals treasures. **Neront** appears in the form of a bird, teaches and heals sickness, stirs up quarrels and makes fools dance. He is invoked on Wednesdays, Fridays and Saturdays during a waxing Moon. **Siviant** speaks truthfully, strengthens the Spirits, and makes sure that [the Spirits] will tell everything [they know]. **Nemon**, only his upper half is in human form, with a long beard, a crown upon his head, gives answers, bestows remembrance and the ability to remember anything that one wishes. **Baal**, a mighty oriental Prince, bestows the gift to make oneself invisible and to be loved by people. **Agerol**, an old man, bestows knowledge of languages, Lordship and wealth, teaches the knowledge of secret things and of Astrology. **Heneral** heals sickness, and teaches the knowledge of healing and poisonous plants. **Johann** (?)[468] bestows the gift to make oneself loved and opens all prisons. **Artis** appears with two crowns and a sword in his hand and bestows favours to all men. **Machin** teaches the power of stones and plants and brings them from the most distant lands in an instant. **Jilbagor** bestows favours from Princes. **Sibos** appears as an angel and makes one wise and courageous. **Gebepl** teaches the language of birds, makes one invisible and catches thieves and murderers. **Zomal** appears as clear waters and makes it rain, when it is so desired. **Canfft** bestows horses for as long as they are needed. **Margolas** quarrels with every man, carries cities and castles away and places them in an

---

[467] It is unusual to find one of the 12 Apostles listed amongst the names of Spirits.
[468] The question mark is in the text – it is possible that the transcriber was unsure whether this is the correct name or not, as it is the name of John the Baptist or John the Evangelist and not John, a devil! But St Peter has also been listed, so there is already a precedent.

arbitrary place. **Sargas** teaches the power of plants stones, bestows health and wealth and makes you invisible. **Gezery** bestows good workers and catches murderers. **Gewar** comes in the form of a maiden **+** teaches all sciences **+** and when desired, appears in the form of a bird.

GENERAL CONJURATION FOR SPIRITS AND THE DEVIL

"In the Name of God the Father **+**, *of the Son* **+** *and of the Holy Ghost* **+**, *rise up and come, ye evil Spirits, through the Power of the King, through the seven herbs in whose halls the Spirits and the Devil are contained and which compels N.N. to appear before me and answer as I desire, and to fulfil that, which I desire, thereafter is power given to him from the East, West, South and North. I pray and command it of you, through the power of which is threefold, eternal and is of the same substance, which is an invisible and unique being. In the Name of the Father* **+** *of the Son* **+** *and of the Holy Ghost* **+** *Amen. Go hence to your place in peace, which is between us and yourselves."*

FIRST CONJURATION: TO THE LORD OF THE EAST

"Oy ey micane and all holy Martyrs, through the Power of the Most High, I command thee to quickly send me N.N. from his dwelling[469] *and answer all my questions, or thou hast to come thyself to do my will and if thou doest not fulfil my wish promptly, then so shall I compel thee through the power of the Almighty God to answer all my questions."*

SECOND CONJURATION: TO THE LORD OF THE WEST

"Raimond, most mighty Prince, thou, who rulest towards the West, I summon thee by all the highest Names of the Godhead, I command thee through the power of the Highest Names to quickly send N.N. hither, so that he may answer and do always what I shall command of him and if thou doest not do this, then so shall I increase thy pain and burn thee."

---

[469] The text is a little confusing here: literally it reads: *"I command thee to send me quickly and our 1 to begin with 2 dwells"*. I am assuming that this is due to an error of copying and so, I am ignoring what I believe to be typos in order to give the best translation possible.

THIRD CONJURATION: TO THE LORD OF THE SOUTH

"Naemon, thou who rulest towards the South, I call upon thee through all the Highest Names of the Godhead, I command thee by the power of All the Highest Names to quickly dispatch N.N. hither, so that he may answer me and do what I shall always command of him, and if thou dost not do this, so shall I compel thee by the Power of the Godly Majesty to do it."

FOURTH CONJURATION: TO THE LORD OF THE NORTH

*"**Agina, Agelissa, Glieta, Brieta, Lutecerus, Rebedin,** I call and conjure thee by the Power of all Powers, not to delay in sending me N.N. in a human and pleasant form, or else thou thyself shalt come in the Name of the Father + of the Son + and of the Holy Ghost + and be thou obedient unto me without any danger to my body or soul. Come in human form, I conjure thee by all the Holy Highest Names to be prepared to come hither, or send N.N.N.N. through the Power of the Living and True God and through the Power that was spoken through me and through whose commandment all things came to be, the Heavens, the Earth, the Waters, the Abyss and all that is within, I conjure thee by the Father + by the Son + by the Holy Ghost + and by the Mother of Jesus Christ, the eternally Holy Virgin, by her Purity and Holiness, by the fruitfulness and usefulness of her virginal body and her breast, by the holy womb and her holy milk, which the Son of the Father suckled of her holy body and through all the holy tears and all the holy sighs at the time of his painful suffering on the beam of the Holy Cross that escaped from his eyes and his breast, by all holy things that have come to pass and are yet to come in Heaven as upon Earth, to the honour of our Lord Jesus Christ and the blessèd Virgin Mary, and all that is hallowed and honoured in the strife-filled Church to the honour of his Holy Name, by the Holy Trinity and by the most precious blood, that flowed from his side and through his Annunciation and his becoming man and his holy baptism and the shaking of the Earth and the sweat[470] that flowed from his body and his [moment of] weakness, in which he said to his Father, "If it is possible, let the bitter cup of death be taken from me"[471] through his heavenly ascension and the sanctuary of the Holy Ghost +."*

---

[470] *"Sweat"* is a euphemism in German for *"blood"*, so this word could be translated as either *"sweat"* or *"blood"* or could even mean both.
[471] See *Matthew 26:39* and *Mark 14:36*.

"I conjure thee anew, by the Crown of Thorns, which he bore upon his head, by his hands and feet and by the nails of his Cross, by his wounds and by the tears, which twice he shed, and by the anguish, which he suffered for us with great love throughout all his holy limbs, by the holy Resurrection, by the swaddling clothes that were wrapped around the baby Jesus, by the fruit, which the Virgin Mary bore in her chaste body, by the Prayers of Intercession of the glorious Virgin Mary, by all the Holy Angels and Archangels, by the nine Superior Spirits, Patriarchs, Apostles and Evangelists, by the Holy Virgin and by the chains and bonds of God, by the Herald John the Baptist, by the science of the Holy Catherine[472] and by all the holy souls."

Note: When this conjuration has been said and the named Spirits have appeared, they must then leave their sign in this book. Before [doing] anything else, you should recite the Gospel of St. John over it, and once again when it is signed. Hereafter, the Spirit must promise that he will come as often as he is called. After this, you may release him, when you have given him something as a gift.

METHOD FOR DISCHARGING SPIRITS

"In the Name of the One, who gives all things a purpose, before whom all knees must bend, who doth not suffer anyone to oppose his Power, by which I compel you to remain fast and firm and not to retreat from here, before ye have fulfilled my will completely, through the power of which have these boundaries been placed around you, past which you may never pass, in the Name of the Creator of all Beings, in the Name of the Father ✝ of the Son ✝ and of the Holy Ghost ✝, return now to your place, may Peace be between us and you, being prepared to reappear, as oft as ye are called upon."

Note: The Pentacle must be consecrated and held up along with the Host during the Mass, before it is aspersed with Holy Water. It is to be shown quickly to the Spirits who show disobedience to our wishes, and say:

---

[472] St Catherine of Alexandria, martyred in the 4th century CE.

"See ye this, the means of your coercion? Be ye not obstinate to our Will and return now to your abodes. May there be peace between us and you and be ye prepared to reappear, as often as ye are called upon."

THE CONJURATION FOR THE DIFFERENT DAYS OF THE WEEK OF THE AFORE-MENTIONED SPIRITS

On **Sunday**: **Aziel**. It is spoken between midnight and 1 o'clock in the morning. When he appears, he will request a strand of hair from your head. You must not, however, give him one of your own, but a strand of hair from someone or something else, perhaps from a hare. He requires it, in order to show you treasures or indeed other things too, about which you wish to ask him.

*"I conjure thee, **Aziel**, by all the Holy Names, which are recorded in this book, to obey me immediately and to send me another Spirit, who will bring me a stone, with which will allow me to speak and neither be heard nor seen by anybody. I conjure thee to show thyself obedient to whomever you are sent and without causing any harm to me, and to fulfil my desires, so that the conditions that I shall make for you, will be known to you."*

On **Monday**: **Lucifer**. The conjuration takes place in the night between 11 o'clock and midnight, or between 3 and 4 o'clock in the morning. The circle is drawn with coal. The conjurer should have Holy Water to hand and should don a surplice.

THE CONJURATION

*"I conjure thee, **Lucifer** by the True God ✝ by the Holy God ✝ by the God ✝ who hath created all things; I conjure thee by the enduring Name of God ✝ **Alpha Omega Eloy Saday Messias** and I conjure, compel and constrain thee by the Holy Names of God, which are made known to you through the characters **V.P.X.**, to immediately issue one of thy Spirits in a pleasing human form and who will give me an answer to all my questions and who will be impotent to cause harm to me, either in body or in soul."*

On **Tuesday**: **Nimrod**. He must be summoned between 9 and 10 o'clock at night. He should be given the first stone that you find.

THE CONJURATION

"I conjure thee, Nimrod[473] *and command thee by all names by which thou mayest be compelled and summoned; I conjure thee Nimrod by all Spirits and by all Creatures, by the Seal of Solomon, which doubles and increases curses and pain upon thee for all time, if thou dost not come and fulfil my will without injury to either my body or soul."*

On **Wednesday**: **Astaroth**. She should be called upon between 10 and 11 o'clock at night. She brings about favours of Princes.

"I conjure thee, **Astaroth** *and command thee by the Power of Jesus of Nazareth, to whom all devils are subservient and who was born of the Virgin Mary through the Mystery of the Angel Gabriel, again I conjure thee in the Name of the Father +* *of the Son +* *and of the Holy Ghost +* *in the Name of the glorious Virgin Mary and of the Holy Trinity, of all Archangels and Thrones, of Dominions and of Powers, Patriarchs and Prophets, Apostles and Evangelists, who do not cease to sing, "Holy, Holy, Holy is the Lord, the God of Hosts, who is like unto a consuming flame, to which thou durst not come." I command thee by the one, who on the Day of Judgement will come with Fire to judge the Quick and the Dead, not to scorn the one, to whom alone all Honour and all Praise is due, appear forthwith and obey my will, give honour to the Holy Ghost, in his Name do I command thee."*

On **Thursday**: **Acham**. He is summoned between 3 and 4 o'clock in the morning; he appears in the form of a King. He should be given some of your own gold to make him speak, to further men's fortunes and to open hidden treasures.

---

[473] Nimrod is mentioned at various times in the Hebrew Scriptures (*Genesis 10:8-12*; *1 Chronicles 1:10* and *Micah 5:6*) as being the son of Cush, the grandson of Ham, and the great grandson of Noah. He was called a *"mighty hunter"* and Jewish tradition states that Nimrod met with Abraham and that there was a great confrontation between them, with Abraham representing good and Nimrod Evil. In fact, Nimrod was said to have stood in direct opposition to God and sets himself up as a god with his own followers.

*"I conjure thee, **Acham**, by the same image and likeness of our Lord Jesus Christ, who through his death hath redeemed the human race, to appear before me forthwith, I command thee by all Kingdoms of God **+ Agios**, I conjure thee by his Holy Name, who treads on lions and dragons into the ground, to execute my will without causing harm to me, either to my body or soul."*

On **Friday**: **Ragiel**. He is called upon between 11 and 12 o'clock at night. He should be given a mouse, so that shows himself to be willing.

*"I conjure thee, **Ragiel** and command thee to come to me, I compel thee by the Names **Elai + Adonai + Eloi + Aglat Taminabot +** and all Holy Names that are recorded in this book, by the most Holy Sacraments of the Altar, by he, who hath redeemed man from his sins, I conjure thee to come immediately, without harm to my body or soul and to execute my command."*

On **Saturday**: **Nabara**. He is summoned between 11 o'clock at night and midnight. As soon as he appears, he should be given some bread and command him to obey.

*"I conjure thee, **Nabara** in the Name of **Satan** and **Beelzebub**, and in the Name of **Astaroth** and all other Spirits to appear before me, when-soever I command it of thee, neither deceiving me nor harming me, either in body nor soul. I command thee to come to me immediately or send another Spirit, who hath the same power, to achieve my wishes and who will no sooner disappear until I have discharged him."*

SIX STRONG CONJURATIONS, BY WHICH THE SPIRITS ARE COMPELLED TO APPEAR TO THE CONJURER AT EVERY APPOINTED TIME AND EXECUTE THE WILL OF THE CONJURER.

"I conjure thee, evil Spirit, thou, who inhabitest this place, in whatever part of the World that thou mayest now also be and whatever kind of Power hath been given thee over this place by God and the Holy Angels, I exorcise thee through the Might of the Father + through the Wisdom of the Son + and through the Strength of the Holy Ghost + through the truth, which is always given by the true Lord Jesus Christ, the Crucified, the Son of the One, who created all creatures, and who hath given you[474] power over this place,

---

[474] The language has again shifted from *"thou/thee"* (singular) to *"ye/you"* (plural) in

therefore do I command you of your own free will, without trickery or deception to tell me your names, through the merit of the glorious Virgin Mary and all Holy Ones do I exorcise you Spirits from this site and I send you into the depths of the Abyss of Hell and I say: "Go hence, ye accursèd Spirits, into the eternal fire, which is prepared for you and all your companions, when-soever ye show yourselves to be disobedient, and I conjure, constrain and command you powerfully, I compel you by the Most Holy Names of God ✛ Aon ✛ Baid ✛ Etar ✛ Seboti ✛ Combin ✛ Atur ✛ Adonai ✛ Hen ✛ Tetragrammaton ✛ Sadai ✛ Messias ✛ Agios ✛ Ischros ✛ Emanuel ✛ Alpha ✛ to have no more power to remain in this place. I command you and forewarn you, as may be befitting to you Devils that the Archangel Michael will cast you into the Prison of Hell in the Name of God the Father ✛ of the Son ✛ and of the Holy Ghost ✛."

Aacoel conceals and gives treasures to whom he wills, his Region is the South. **Sabiel**, Spirit of Wealth, collects and donates it to whom he wills, his Region is the East. **Achariel** creates gold and silver, his Region is the South. **Odail** teaches sciences, his Region is the North. **Nadel**, Spirit of court trials, he issues summons to the sentences, he dwells towards the South. **Anasta**, Spirit of Love between man and woman, he brings it into existence and preserves it. He lives towards the South. **Masiel**, Spirit of warlords, he instils courage and vigour and rules towards the West. **Posses** rules in fields, chases the foe in the air and ministers towards the South. **Azdical**, Spirit of the Arts, ministers towards the West. **Oriel** rules over the sea and makes it still again, he dwells towards the East. **Heleniert** provides favours and privileged positions, he lives towards the South. **Namut**, Patron of Thieves, can be of help but he is also [Patron] to lost things. **Zaral**, Spirit of Forests, favours those who love hunting, he operates towards the North. **Ramaloth** opens prisons, he operates towards the South.

End of the Grimoire as authored by Pope Honorius the Great

Anno **1220**.

---

the text – although the German keeps the *"ihr/euch"* (you plural familiar) forms, which is not expressed at all in Early Modern and Modern English.

APPENDIX TO THE SCHEIBLE EDITION

(This appendix is found attached to the German Version of the Grimoire of Pope Honorius.)

The Handwritten Chapter[475]

"I sign and swear by my Sigil, which is placed at the end of this truthful manuscript, firstly, that I the same [Spirit], who[se name] is found in this Book, [will appear] at once and immediately in a pleasing human form and without any uproar, without any deception and without any flashes of fire, [and I] will bring, whatever he so desires, in whatever language and in any manner that the conjurer wants, [I swear] that I shall bring him what he desires."

*"**Ingera zanium** [I swear] by my word."*

*"**Polum pollum** and as many that dwell here, to judge and promise, [I swear] to bring wise Spirits, which this book contains or which are written within, to the persons [so requesting them]."*

*"**Quollum opium** [I shall appear] in whatever form is required of me, [and bring] gold or silver made by men's hands, to be used when needed for any commercial opportunity, [and bring it] to wherever the conjurer may live; so without delay I shall bring him what he desires, so that he may be able to run his business, buy and sell, build and demolish and anything else that he may want do to at his own pleasure."*

"Furthermore, I undertake to freely and willingly deliver the so-desired treasures to the conjurer, whether they be concealed in the depths of the Earth or in the Abysses of the Sea, I also promise to transform old coins into usable foreign currency, whatever may be in current use where the conjurer lives."

"Finally, I vow to protect the owner of this written Book, from all dangers, from his enemies' pursuits, to preserve his health and to bear his sorrows, so that he is never called

---

[475] Note from the Trident Edition p. 30 *"This section is an Oath which the spirit is to mark with his sign or sigil. This section, although unrelated to The Grimoire of Pope Honorius, was appended to the original manuscript which was originally acquired by Mr. Scheible."*

before the courts of law. When he is travelling, I will escort him and ensure that he covers his journey quickly and without trouble; I shall appear to him in a human form and speak to him in his habitual language, allow his knowledge to increase, so that he may understand everything that he reads, fulfil all wishes without exception, without trickery or deception, without causing harm to either his life nor soul and nothing shall ever again be wrested from him nor shall any evil be inflicted upon him. To reaffirm this, to which I am hereto avowed, I have enclosed my Sigil and Signature."

SUMMONS:[476]

+++   *"Come forthwith without delay, my King Meridial and appear to me in a human and pleasing form and serve me, as thou hast sworn. Make haste, hurry and execute my wishes."*

LICENSE TO DEPART:

"Go in peace to the place, that God hath intended for thee, and retreat in haste from me, but appear quickly, where and when I shall require it of thee, without uproar or inflicting harm to my body or soul, to my reason or five senses."

"As has been said above, neither [inflict harm] to those, who may be with me and thou shouldst preserve me from all that is harmful."

END

---

[476] The three crosses are to the left of the Summons. The whole summons is indented.

CONCLUDING REMARK

If you want to summon a Treasure Spirit, gather some earth during the hour of the Full Moon, in particularly [gather] three spoonfuls of earth with a new pewter spoon [and place it] on a new sheet of paper and say:

"In the Name of the Father do I seek thee, in the Name of the Son do I find thee, in the Name of the Holy Ghost do I compel thee, and in the Name of the Holy Trinity do I command thee to appear visibly with thy concealed goods and to leave me that, which I desire from thee in the place, from where I have [taken] this earth, in the name of N. + + +."

"Ego adjuro te custodem hujus thesauri in hoc loco a quo terram habeo per schalzo Goreb Agla siosmas nacus gaddurus et ulla odoi sabarlitt amara et miheline omni mora in spesi aprexum signo terribilem fac onri damno et issione corporis et animæ visibiliter comburens et omnibus maudalis meis obtemperes. Amen +++."[477]

THE EXORCISM:

"Thou Spirit and evil soul! I bind and conjure thee with these Words of Power, through which Solomon conjured and banished the Spirits, by **Tetragrammaton Agla Mothom** *principa moritura maschilam corporis maschilam in facto.'*[478]

Speak thrice: *"Siko alam aca.'*[479]

DISMISSAL:

Speak thrice: *"masar Rader Risie isuam polmarasi test mar ofa.'*[480]

---

[477] This passage seems to be a mixture of Latin and barbarous or corrupted words: *"I charge thee, guardian of the treasures of the earth of this place have the schalzo Goreb Egla siosmas nacus gaddurus and ulla odoi sabarlitt bitter and miheline any delay in the hope aprexum and make a terrible loss and onri issione visibly burning his body and soul and obey all my maudalis. Amen".*

[478] This is again Latin with an unknown word, *"maschilam"*, so tentatively it may be interpreted as *"By the origin of death I shall [maschilam] from the body I shall in fact [maschilam]".* In the context of the Exorcism a possible interpretation might be a corruption of a word meaning *'overcome'* or something similar, but we have found nothing which supports this.

[479] A barbarous phrase.

[480] Another barbarous phrase.

TO THE GENTLE READER!

What has been presented is a faithful extract from the printed Book of the Great Grimoire, without any of the useless and frivolous passages being omitted. So, a pious Priest, on whom God has bestowed insight and grace, should get this book into his possession, so he may compel the evil Spirits mentioned in the above procedure[481] to leave his signature [in this Book] and he will be placed in a position to be able to usefully assist many people.

When the Priest christens [the Book], he should smear and bend back the corners of the Book with some Chrism[482] in three places, so that the corners will not be touched by anyone's hands and also, for greater precaution, stick Host wafers to the corners while reading the Mass both for the Exorcism and the Conjuration in the order as stated.

Firstly, before the three-day fast of bread and water begins, the Mass in honour of the Holy Trinity must be read over this Book, then the Priest can baptise it.

The prepared Pentacle must be set in place by him beforehand. He should asperse it with Holy Water mixed with centaury.

How to summon the Spirits of the Air has been shown previously. It is also good to read a *Holy Mass to the Holy Ghost*. During the following night, the Priest begins his *Mass of Coercion* along with the prayers, as have been set down here in Latin. Then [perform] the Conjuration ritual using the prayers, then when the pastor needs obedience from the Spirit, perform the other Conjurations, to which the Spirit has added his signature. Before the Spirit is discharged, he should be given something for his troubles. The Priest should read this *Mass of Coercion* for as many nights as it is necessary for the Spirit to finally appear. Then he speaks with the Spirit, as a Lord speaks to his servant, fearless and firm, then the Spirit can inflict him no harm. You are cautioned to read through the booklet many times, so that no error can slip into the order of proceedings.

Laudetur Jesus Christus![483]

---

[481] The word is *"Form"*, probably an abbreviation for *"Formel"*, which is a formula or even ceremony

[482] Chrism is holy anointing oil.

[483] *"Praised be Jesus Christ!"* This is also a traditional greeting between members of the clergy of the Roman Catholic Church.

MATERIAL FROM THE GRIMOIRE OF POPE HONORIUS DUPLICATED IN LATER GRIMOIRES

	GoPH 1670	Grimorium Verum		Black Dragon
Conjuration of the Book	Yes			Yes
Conjuration of the Demons	Yes			Yes
Conjuration of the King of the East	Yes			Yes
Conjuration of the King of the South	Yes			Yes
Conjuration of the King of the West	Yes			Yes
Conjuration of the King of the North	Yes			Yes
For Monday to Lucifer	Yes			Yes
For Tuesday to Frimost	Yes			Yes
For Wednesday to Astaroth	Yes			Yes
For Thursday to Silcharde	Yes	Yes		Yes
For Friday to Bechard	Yes	Yes		Yes
For Saturday to Guland	Yes	Yes		Yes
For Sunday to Surgat	Yes	Yes		Yes
Very Powerful Conjuration for all days and all hours, Day and Night, for treasures hidden by men as well as Spirits, to have them or have them transported	Yes			Yes
Charm	GoPH 1670	Grimorium Verum	Grand Grimoire	Black Dragon
To see spirits, of which the air is replete	Yes	Yes		

233

To make three ladies or three gentlemen come to your room after supper	Yes	Yes	Yes	
To make a girl come find you, no matter how wise she may be	Yes	Yes	Yes	Yes
To win at games	Yes			Yes
In order to extinguish a chimney fire	Yes	Yes		
To make oneself invisible	Yes	Yes	Yes	Yes
To get gold and silver, or a Hand of Glory	Yes	Yes	Yes*	Yes*
Garter in order to travel without tiring oneself / To succeed on a journey	Yes	Yes	Yes	Yes
To make a girl dance naked	Yes	Yes	Yes	Yes
To see a vision in the night of what you wish to see, in the past or the future	Yes	Yes		Yes
To use a nail to make someone suffer	Yes	Yes		Yes
To make oneself appear to be accompanied by many	Yes			Yes
Not to be wounded by any weapon	Yes			Yes
To enjoy the use of whomever you wish. Secret of Father Girard	Yes	Yes		
To make a weapon fail	Yes			Yes
Against a sword strike	Yes			Yes
For when you are going into action	Yes			Yes
For burns	Yes			Yes
To prevent someone eating at the table	Yes			Yes
To prevent copulation	Yes			Yes
To win at games	Yes			Yes
To stop a serpent in its tracks	Yes			Yes
For games of dice	Yes			Yes

Not to tire of walking	Yes	Yes		
To avoid interrogation	Yes		Yes	
The Great Exorcism to dispossess either the human creature or irrational animals	Yes			Yes
To remove all spells and to summon the person who caused the evil deed	Yes			Yes
The Castle of the Fair, a guard for horses	Yes			Yes
To stop horses and carriages	Yes			Yes
Secret to discover treasures	Yes	Yes		
Counter-Charm	Yes			Yes
For the lambs to return beautiful and very strong	Yes			Yes
Protection against all firearms	Yes			Yes
For glanders and colic in horses	Yes			Yes

EDITIONS OF THE GRIMOIRE OF POPE HONORIUS

Rome, 1670

Gremoire du Pape Honorius; avec un recueil des plus rares secrets.

Rome, 1670[B]

Le Grimoire du Pape Honorius; avec un recueil des plus grandes secrets de l'art magique et des pratiques s'opposant aux malefices

Wellcome 4666, Paris?, Mid-18th century

Le Veritable Grimoire du Pape Honorius

BL 8632.a.3. Rome, [Paris?] 1760

Grimoire du Pape Honorius, avec un recueil des plus rares secrets.

BL 8630.aa.21. Rome, [Paris?] 1800

Grimoire du Pape Honorius; avec un recueil des plus grands secrets.

de Plancy, 1825, 1670 French text reproduced in *Dictionnaire Infernal Vol 2*

Scheible, 1845-1849, reproduced in *Das Kloster*, Band III, pp634-662

Der Gross Grimoir Des Papis Honorius

Waite, 1898, English translation of 1760 French edition (first part) reproduced in *The Book of Black Magic*

The Grimoire of Honorius, in chapter entitled *The Method of Honorius*

Fidi (ed), 1924, Italian translation of 1760 French edition

Il Grimorio di Papa Onorio III

Shah, 1957, English translation of 1760 French edition (first part) reproduced in *The Secret Lore of Magic*

The Grimoire of Honorius the Great

Dumas, 1972 (2008 reprint), French reprint of 1670 French edition (first part) in *Grimoires et Rituels Magiques*

Le Livre des Conjurations du Pape Honorius

Unnamed, 1970, French reprint of the 1670 edition

Le Livre des Conjurations du Pape Honorius. Avec un recueil des plus rare Secrets de l'Art Magique et des pratiques s'opposant aux maléfices.

King (trans), 1984, English translation of 1760 French edition (first part)

The Grimoire of Pope Honorius III

Ch'ien (trans), 1998, English translation of German from *Das Kloster*

The Great Grimoire of Pope Honorius

Rolland, E.N., 1879, reproduction of the Guidon material

Faune populaire de la France: Tome II - Les Oiseaux Saivages - Noms Vulgaires, Dictons, Proverbes, Legendes, Contes et Superstitions

Guidon, & Pissier (trans), 2011, English translation of the Guidon material

Magic Secrets

BIBLIOGRAPHY

Agrippa, Cornelius, & Tyson, D. (ed) (2005) *Three Books of Occult Philosophy*. Minnesota: Llewellyn

Agrippa, Cornelius, et al (2005) *The Fourth Book of Occult Philosophy*. Maine: Ibis Press

Anon (1909) *Le Dragon Noir Ou Les Forces Infernales Soumises à L'homme*. Paris: Librairie Générale Des Sciences Occultes

Blanchard, R. (1996) *The Black Dragon*. California: IGOS

Boudet, Jean-Patrice (2003) *Les who's who démonologiques de la Renaissance et leurs ancêtres médiévaux*. In *Médiévales* 44:117-140

Brucker, Gene A. (1963) *Sorcery in Early Renaissance Florence*. In *Studies in the Renaissance* Vol. 10:7-24

Butler, E.M. (1980) *Ritual Magic*. Cambridge: Cambridge University Press

Ch'ien, Rineta (trans), & Sullivan, Matthew (1998) *The Great Grimoire of Pope Honorius*. Washington: Trident Books

Coe, J.B. & Young, S. (ed., trans.) (1995) *The Celtic Sources for the Arthurian Legend*. Felinfach: Llanerch Press

Couliano, Ioan P. (1987) *Eros and Magic in the Renaissance*. Chicago: Chicago University Press

D'Aban, Pierre (1744) *Les Oeuvres Magiques d'Henri Corneille Agrippa*. Paris: Liege

Davies, Owen (2009) *Grimoires: A History of Magic Books*. Oxford: Oxford University Press

Davies, Owen (2004) *French Charmers and their Healing Charms*. In *Charms and Charming in Europe*. Basingstoke: Palgrave Macmillan

Davies, Owen (2003) *Cunning-Folk: Popular Magic in English History*. New York: Hambledon & London

De Givery, E.G. (1931) *Sorcery, Magic and Alchemy*. London: George G.

Harrap & Co. Ltd

D'Este, Sorita & Rankine, David (2008) *Wicca Magickal Beginnings: A Study of the Possible Origins of the Rituals and Practices Found in this Modern Tradition of Pagan Witchcraft and Magick*. London: Avalonia

Devlin, Judith (1987) *The Superstitious Mind: French Peasants and the Supernatural in the Nineteenth Century*. Glasgow: Bell & Bain Ltd

Dumas, F.R. (2008) *Grimoires et Rituels Magiques*. Paris: Le Pre aux Clercs

Eamon, William (1994) *Science and the Secrets of Nature: Books of Secrets in Medieval and Early Modern Culture*. Princeton: Princeton University Press

Fanger, Claire (2012) *Invoking Angels, Theurgic Ideas and Practices, Thirteenth to Sixteenth Century*. Pennsylvania: Pennsylvania State Press

Fanger, Claire (ed) (1998) *Conjuring Spirits: Texts and Traditions of Medieval Ritual Magic*. Stroud: Sutton Publishing Ltd

Flowers, Stephen (1989) *The Galdabrok. An Icelandic Grimoire*. Maine: Samuel Weiser Inc

Forbes, Thomas R. (1971) *Verbal Charms in British Folk Medicine*. In *Proceedings of the American Philosophical Society* Vol. 115.4:293-316

French, Sarah K. (trans) (2004) *The Enchiridion of Pope Leo III*.

Gardner, Gerald B. (1954) *Witchcraft Today*. London: Rider & Co.

Gardner, Gerald B. (1959) *The Meaning of Witchcraft*. London: Aquarian

Grendon, Felix (1909) *The Anglo-Saxon Charms*. In *The Journal of American Folklore* Vol 22.84:105-237

Guidon & Pissier, P. (trans) (2011) *Magic Secrets*. Hinckley, Society for Esoteric Endeavour

Hedegård, Gösta (2002) *Liber Iuratus Honorii*. Stockholm: Almquist & Wiksell International

Hohman, J.G. (1820) *Pow-wows; or, Long Lost Friend: A Collection of Mysterious and Invaluable Arts and Remedies, for Man as well as Animals, with many Proofs*. Pennsylvania: Hohman

Hughes, G. (1750) *The Natural History of Barbados*. London

Kieckhefer, Richard (2001) *Magic in the Middle Ages*. Cambridge: Cambridge University Press

King, B.J.H. (trans) (1984) *The Grimoire of Pope Honorius III*.

Northampton: Sut Anubis Books

Lea, H.C. (1957) *Materials Towards A History Of Witchcraft* (3 volumes). New York: Thomas Yoseloff

Lecouteux, Claude (2002) *Le Livres des Grimoires.* Paris: Editions Imago

Lehrich, C.I. (2003) *The Language of Demons and Angels: Cornelius Agrippa's Occult Philosophy.* Leiden: Brill

Levi, Eliphas (1913) *The History of Magic.* London: William Rider & Son

Levi, Eliphas (1959) *The Key of the Mysteries.* London: Rider & Co.

Longenbach, James (1988) *Stone Cottage: Pound, Yeats & Modernism.* Oxford: Oxford University Press

Marathakis, Ioannis (2007) *From the Ring of Gyges to the Black Cat Bone - A Historical Survey of the Invisibility Spells.* http://www.hermetics.org/Invisibilitas.html

Meller, W.C. (1925) *Old Times. Relics, Talismans, forgotten customs & beliefs of the past.* London: T. Werner Laurie

Michaud, L.G. (1865) *Biographie Universelle Ancienne et Moderne XIV.* Paris: Delagrave & Co

Mollenauer, Lynn Wood (2007) *Strange Revelations: Magic, Poison, and Sacrilege in Louis XIV's France.* Pennsylvania: Pennsylvania State University Press

Monter, William (1997) *Toads and Eucharists: The Male Witches of Normandy, 1564-1660.* In *French Historical Studies* Vol 20.4:563-595

Murray, J. (1877) *The Academy*, issue 12. London

Nash, J.R. (1990) *Encyclopedia of World Crime Vol IV S-Z Supplements.* Illinois: CrimeBooks Inc

Nowotny, K.A. (1949) *The Construction of Certain Seals and Characters in the Work of Agrippa of Nettesheim.* In *Journal of the Warburg and Courtauld Institutes* Vol 12:46-57

Paracelsus & Skinner, Stephen (ed) (1975) *The Archidoxes of Magic.* London: Askin

Peterson, Joseph (ed) (2001) *The Lesser Key of Solomon: Lemegeton Clavicula Salomonis.* Maine: Weiser Books

Peterson, Joseph H. (ed, trans) (2007) *Grimorium Verum.* California:

CreateSpace

Putzel, Steven (1986) *Reconstructing Yeats: The Secret Rose and The Wind Among the Reeds.* Dublin: Gill & Macmillan Ltd

Rankine, David (2009) *The Book of Treasure Spirits.* London: Avalonia

Rankine, David & Barron, Harry (trans) (2009) *A Collection of Magical Secrets.* London: Avalonia

Rolland, E.N. (1879) *Faune populaire de la France: Tome II - Les Oiseaux Saivages - Noms Vulgaires, Dictons, Proverbes, Legendes, Contes et Superstitions.* Paris: Maisonneuve & cie

Roper, Jonathan (ed) (2004) *Charms and Charming in Europe.* Basingstoke: Palgrave Macmillan

Ryan, W.F. (1995) *The Bathhouse at Midnight: Magic in Russia.* Stroud: Sutton Publishing Ltd

Scheible, Johann (1845-49) *Das Kloster: Weltlich und geistlich. Meist aus der ältern deutschen Volks-, Wunder-, Curiositäten-, und vorzugsweise komischen Literatur,* in 12 volumes

Scot, Reginald (1584) *Discoverie of Witchcraft.* London

Shah, Idries (1969) *The Secret Lore of Magic.* London: Frederick Muller Ltd

Shah, Sirdar Ikbal Ali (1952) *Occultism: Its Theory and Practice.* New York: Castle Books

Simon (2007) *Papal Magic, Occult Practices Within the Catholic Church.* New York: Harper

Skemer, Don C. (2006) *Binding Words: Textual Amulets in the Middle Ages.* Penn State Press: Pennsylvania

Skinner, Stephen & Rankine, David (2007) *The Goetia of Dr Rudd.* Singapore: Golden Hoard Press

Skinner, Stephen & Rankine, David, & Barron, Harry (trans) (2008) *The Veritable Key of Solomon.* Singapore: Golden Hoard Press

Taillepied, Noël (1588) *Traicté de l'apparition des esprits.* Paris: G Bichon

Thompson, C.J.S. (1927) *Mysteries and Secrets of Magic.* London: John Lane

Thorndike, Lynn (1923) *A History of Magical and Experimental Science Vol*

2. New York: Columbia University Press

Traimond, Bernard (1988) *Le pouvoir de la maladie: Magie et politique dans les Landes de Gascogne 1750–1826.* Bordeaux: Université de Bordeaux

Waite, A.E. (1911) *The Book of Ceremonial Magic.* London: William Rider & Son

Waite, A.E. (1886) *The Mysteries of Magic: A Digest of the Writings of Eliphas Levi.* London: George Redway

INDEX

Other titles from Avalonia....

A Collection of Magical Secrets by David Rankine (editor)

Artemis: Virgin Goddess of the Sun & Moon by Sorita d'Este

Defences Against the Witches' Craft by John Canard

From a Drop of Water (anthology, various contributors) edited by Kim Huggens

Heka: Egyptian Magic by David Rankine

Hekate Her Sacred Fires (anthology) edited by Sorita d'Este

Hekate Liminal Rites (history) by Sorita d'Este & David Rankine

Memento Mori (anthology) by Kim Huggens (editor)

Odin's Gateways by Katie Gerrard

Seidr: The Gate is Open by Katie Gerrard

Stellar Magic by Payam Nabarz

The Book of Gold by David Rankine (editor) & Paul Harry Barron (translator)

The Cosmic Shekinah by Sorita d'Este & David Rankine

The Faerie Queens (anthology, various contributors), edited by Sorita d'Este and David Rankine

The Gods of the Vikings by Marion Pearce

The Grimoire of Arthur Gauntlet by David Rankine (editor)

The Guises of the Morrigan by David Rankine & Sorita d'Este

The Isles of the Many Gods by David Rankine & Sorita d'Este

The Priory of Sion by Jean-luc Chaumeil

The Temple of Hekate by Tara Sanchez

Thoth: The Ancient Egyptian God of Wisdom by Lesley Jackson

Thracian Magic by Georgi Mishev

Visions of the Cailleach by Sorita d'Este & David Rankine

Vs. (anthology, various contributors) edited by Kim Huggens

Wicca Magickal Beginnings by Sorita d'Este & David Rankine

These and many other books on magic, mysticism and mythology are available from our website: **www.avaloniabooks.co.uk**